Fun & Original
Cakes
for Men & Boys

Fun & Original Cakes
for Men & Boys

Maisie Parrish

David and Charles

www.bakeme.com

To my Italian friend *Sandra Rozza* – we will do great things together. With special thanks to *Vittorio* and *Marco*, and all of Maisie's team in Italy.

IMPORTANT NOTE

The models in this book were made using metric measurements. Imperial conversions have been provided, but the reader is advised that these are approximate and therefore significantly less precise than using the metric measurements given. By means of example, using metric a quantity of 1g can easily be measured, whereas the smallest quantity given in imperial on most modern electric scales is ⅛oz. The author and publisher cannot therefore be held responsible for any errors incurred by using the imperial measurements in this book and advise the reader to use the metric equivalents wherever possible.

Contents

Rock 'n' Roll

King of DIY

Domestic Bliss

Father's Day

Whole Nine Yards

Let It Snow

Hobby-Mad Minis

Introduction

My 'Fun & Original' series has a serious following, and I am very pleased with the cakes I have designed for your enjoyment in this edition. They are quite different from the usual cakes for men – nothing risque, just humorous and charming. Men are notoriously difficult to design for, but you are sure to find something perfect for the special man in your life within these pages.

As usual, my cakes have a lot of detail but don't let that put you off, because you can easily select a few of the things you like to create a simplified design. All the time and effort you put into it will be rewarded when you see him smile, because humour is such an important part of my work.

The materials used for modelling in this series are very simple – just sugarpaste (rolled fondant) with a pinch of CMC (Tylose) added to keep your figures upright – a combination that is very easy to work with.

The thing that links these cakes together is the figures, which is what I am most known for. I pay a great deal of attention to facial expression because a face can convey whatever emotion you wish, so getting that expression right is crucial. The shape of the face, the eyes, nose and mouth are all part of a character, with its own individuality. Even animals have expressions – happy, sad, pathetic or cute – and you can capture it all if you put your mind to it.

The figures on these cakes are about 13cm (5in) in height and the body is usually the size of a golf ball. Sometimes they need to be a

little larger, but the first piece you create – the body – will determine the finished size of the figure. Getting the proportions right is difficult when you first begin modelling. I do give weights and measurements where possible to help guide you with this initially, but as you become more experienced, you will be able to feel if the amount of paste in your hand is too big or too small.

Enjoy!

Maisie

Sugarpaste

All the models in this book are made using sugarpaste (rolled fondant) in one form or another. This firm, sweet paste is also used to cover cakes and boards. Sugarpaste is very soft and pliable and marks very easily, but for modelling it works best if you add CMC (Tylose) to it to bulk it up (see Sugarpaste for Modelling). This section gives you the lowdown on this wonderful medium, revealing everything you need to know for success with sugarpaste.

Ready-Made Sugarpaste

You can purchase sugarpaste in the most amazing array of colours; just take it out of the packet and away you go. Of all the ready-made pastes on the market, the brand leader is Renshaws Regalice (see Suppliers), which is available in white and lots of other exciting shades. This paste is easy to work with and is of excellent firm quality.

Tip

Very dark colours, such as black, dark blue and brown, are particularly useful to buy ready-coloured, because if you add enough paste food colouring into white to obtain a strong shade, it will alter the consistency of the paste and make it much more difficult to work with.

Ready-made packaged sugarpaste is quick and convenient to use. Well-known brands are high quality and give consistently good results.

Making Your Own

While the ready-made sugarpaste is excellent, you can, of course, make your own at home. The bonus of this is that you can then tint your paste to any colour you like using edible paste food colour (see Colouring Sugarpaste). This can then be dusted with edible dust food colour to intensify or soften the shade.

Sugarpaste Recipe

* 900g (2lb) sifted icing (confectioners') sugar
* 120ml (8tbsp) liquid glucose
* 15g (½oz) gelatin
* 15ml (1tbsp) glycerine
* 45ml (3tbsp) cold water

1 Sprinkle the gelatin over the cold water and allow to 'sponge'. Place over a bowl of hot water and stir with a wooden spoon until all the gelatin crystals have dissolved. Do not allow the gelatin mixture to boil.

2 Add the glycerine and glucose to the gelatin and water and stir until melted.

3 Add the liquid mixture to the sifted icing (confectioners') sugar and mix thoroughly until combined.

4 Dust the work surface lightly with icing (confectioners') sugar, then turn out the paste and knead to a soft consistency until smooth and free of cracks.

5 Wrap the sugarpaste completely in cling film or store in an airtight freezer bag. If the paste is too soft and sticky to handle, work in a little more icing (confectioners') sugar.

Quick Sugarpaste Recipe

* 500g (1lb 1½oz) sifted icing (confectioners') sugar
* 1 egg white
* 30ml (2tbsp) liquid glucose

1 Place the egg white and liquid glucose in a clean bowl. Add the icing (confectioners') sugar and mix together with a wooden spoon, then use your hands to bring the mixture into a ball.

2 Follow steps 4 and 5 of the above recipe for kneading and storage.

Sugarpaste is such a versatile modelling medium, it can be used to create an almost endless variety of cute characters.

Sugarpaste for Modelling

To convert sugarpaste into modelling paste, all you need to do is add CMC (Tylose) powder (see Essential Purchases) to the basic recipe. The quantity needed will vary according to the temperature and humidity of the room, so you may need to experiment to get the right mix depending on the conditions you are working in. As a guide, add roughly 5ml (1tsp) of CMC (Tylose) to 225g (8oz) of sugarpaste and knead well. Place inside a freezer bag and allow the CMC (Tylose) to do its work for at least two hours. Knead the paste well before use to warm it up with your hands; this will make it more pliable and easier to use.

If you need to make any modelled parts slightly firmer, for example if they need to support other parts, knead a little extra CMC (Tylose) into the sugarpaste.

Throughout this book I have used the combination of sugarpaste and CMC (Tylose) powder, and find it works very well. If you add too much CMC (Tylose) to the paste it will begin to crack, which is not desirable. Should this happen, knead in a little white vegetable fat (shortening) to soften the paste and make it pliable again.

Colouring Sugarpaste

Whether you choose to make your own, or to buy ready-made sugarpaste, the white variety of both forms can be coloured with paste food colours to provide a wonderful spectrum of shades.

Solid Colours

1 Roll the sugarpaste to be coloured into a smooth ball and run your palm over the top. Take a cocktail stick (toothpick) and dip it into the paste food colour. Apply the colour over the surface of the sugarpaste. Do not add too much at first, as you can always add more if required.

2 Dip your finger into some cooled boiled water, shaking off any excess and run it over the top of the colour. This will allow the colour to disperse much more quickly into the sugarpaste.

3 Dust the work surface with a little icing (confectioners') sugar and knead the colour evenly into the sugarpaste.

4 The colour will deepen slightly as it stands. If you want to darken it even more, just add more paste food colour and knead again.

Marbled Effect

1 Apply the paste food colour to the sugarpaste as directed above, but instead of working it until the colour is evenly dispersed, knead it for a shorter time to give a marbled effect.

2 You can also marble two or more colours into a sausage shape, twist them together and then roll into a ball. Again, do not blend them together too much. Cakes and boards look particularly nice when covered with marbled paste.

Tip

When colouring white sugarpaste, do not use liquid food colour as it will make the paste too sticky.

Edible food colours come in a wide variety of forms – liquid, paste, dust and even pens – all of which can be used to add colour and life to your sugarpaste models.

Painting on Sugarpaste

There are various different ways of painting on sugarpaste. The most common way is to use paste food colour diluted with some cooled boiled water, or you can use liquid food colours and gels. There are also some food colour pens available, but these tend to work better on harder surfaces. Another way is to dilute dust food colour with clear alcohol; this is particularly useful if you want it to dry quickly. Just wash your paintbrush in clean water when you have finished.

Brushes

To paint facial features I use no.00 or no.000 sable paintbrushes. The finer and better quality the brush, the better job you will make of it. To dust the cheeks of my figures I use a cosmetics brush, which has a sponge at one end and a brush at the other. For less detailed work, you can use a variety of sable brushes in different widths.

This Teddy boy is given extra shimmer with wonderful shades of Rainbow Dust. His jacket is dusted with starlight laser lemon and the toggle of his bootlace tie is dusted with jewel fire red.

Storing Sugarpaste

Sugarpaste will always store best wrapped tightly in a freezer bag, making sure you have removed as much air as possible, and then placed in an airtight container to protect it from atmospheric changes. It should be kept out of the sunlight and away from any humidity, in a cool, dry area at least 50cm (20in) off the ground. If the paste has become too dry to work with, knead in some white vegetable fat (shortening). The main thing to remember with any paste is to keep it dry, cool and sealed from the air, as this will make it dry out and go hard.

Food colour pens can be used to add quick and simple embellishments. The stitch marks on this baseball-themed mini cake were drawn on with pens, as they are cleaner and easier to use than liquid food colours.

Liquid food colour is a great way to add details, such as the markings on this dog and the pattern on the wallpaper, which were added with a fine paintbrush.

Modelling

Mastering modelling with sugarpaste is the key to creating professional-looking cakes. This section reveals all the tools and techniques you need to help sharpen your modelling skills.

General Equipment

There is a myriad of tools on the market for cake decorating and sugarcraft, but many of them are simply unnecessary. The following list gives my recommended essentials, and these are the items that form the basic tool kit listed in each of the projects in this book.

★ **Large non-stick rolling pin**
For rolling out sugarpaste and marzipan.

★ **Wooden spacing rods (1)**
For achieving an even thickness when rolling out sugarpaste – available in various thicknesses.

★ **Two cake smoothers with handles (2)**
For smoothing sugarpaste when covering cakes – use two smoothers together for a professional finish.

★ **Flower former (3)**
For placing delicate parts in while working on them so that they do not lose their shape.

★ **Paint palette (4)**
For mixing liquid food colour or dust food colour and clear alcohol in for painting on sugarpaste.

★ **Quality sable paintbrushes (5)**
For painting on sugarpaste and for modelling – used mainly for painting facial features and applying edible glue. The end of a paintbrush can be pushed into models to create nostrils, used to curl laces of paste around to make curly tails or hair, and used to open up flower petals.

★ **Textured rolling pins (6)**
For creating decorative patterns in paste – for example, rice textured, daisy patterned and ribbed (see Texturing Sugarpaste).

★ **Pastry brush (7)**
For painting apricot glaze and clear spirits onto fruit cakes.

★ **Cutting wheel (8)**
For making smooth cuts on long pieces of sugarpaste, for use on borders mainly. A pizza cutter can be used instead.

Plastic marzipan knife
For trimming the edges of cakes and boards for a neat result.

Sugar press (9)
For extruding lengths of paste to make grass, wool, fluff and hair –a standard garlic press, found in all kitchens, is very effective for this.

Plunger cutters (10)
For cutting out different shapes in sugarpaste – such as daisies, hearts, stars and flowers.

Good-quality stainless steel cutters
Round, square, rectangle, butterfly, heart, petal/blossom – in assorted sizes. For cutting out clean shapes for use in decorations.

Frilling tool
For making frills in sugarpaste and sugar flower paste pieces – a cocktail stick (toothpick) can be used instead.

Cake cards
For placing sugarpaste models on while working on them before transferring them to the cake.

Mini turntable (11)
Useful for placing a cake on so that it can be turned around easily while working on it – not essential.

Measuring cups (12)
For measuring out powders and liquids quickly and cleanly.

Flower stamens (13)
For creating whiskers or antennae on sugarpaste animals and insects.

Non-stick flexi mat
For placing over modelled parts to prevent them drying out – freezer bags can be used instead.

Cake boards (14)
For giving support to the finished cake – 12mm (½in) thickness is ideal.

Specific Modelling Tools

A whole book could be filled talking about these, as there are so many different varieties available. However, I use the white plastic set that has a number on each tool. I refer to the number on the tool throughout the book. They are inexpensive, light and easy to work with, and are available to buy from my website (see Suppliers).

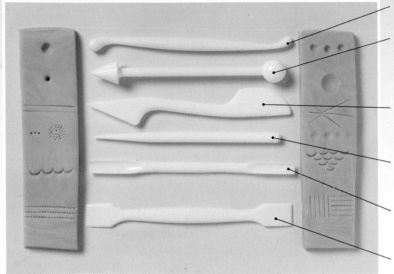

No.1 – bone tool – used to put the ears on animals.

No.3 – tapered cone/ball tool – the pointed end is used for hollowing out the bottom of sleeves and legs, making holes in the tops of bottles etc.

No.4 – knife tool – for cutting and marking fingers and toes.

No.5 – small pointed tool – used for nostrils and making holes.

No.11 – smiley tool – invaluable for marking mouths, eyelids and fish scales.

No.12 – double-ended serrated tool – for adding stitch marks on teddy bears etc.

Securing and Supporting Your Models

Sugarpaste models need to be held together in several ways. Small parts can be attached with edible glue (see Recipes), but larger parts, such as heads and arms, will require additional support.

Throughout the book I use pieces of dry spaghetti for this purpose. The spaghetti is inserted into the models – into the hip, shoulder or body, for example – onto which you can attach another piece – the leg, arm or head. Leave 2cm (¾in) showing at the top to support the head, and 1cm (⅜in) to support arms and legs.

The pieces will still require some edible glue to bond them, but will have more support and will stay rigid. When inserting spaghetti to support heads, make sure that it is pushed into the body in a very vertical position otherwise the head will tilt backwards and become vulnerable.

I recommend using dry raw spaghetti because it is food and is much safer than using cocktail sticks (toothpicks), which could cause harm, particularly to children. However, I would always advise that any spaghetti pieces used are removed before eating the cake and decorations.

Sugarpaste models sometimes need to be supported with foam or cardboard while they are drying to prevent parts from flopping over or drooping down. Advice on where this may be necessary is given in the project instructions.

Basic Shapes

There are four basic shapes required for modelling. Every character in this book begins with a ball; this shape must be rolled first, regardless of whatever shape you are trying to make.

Ball

The first step is always to roll a ball. We do this to ensure that we have a perfectly smooth surface, with no cracks or creases.

For example:

If you pull out the ball at the front, you can shape it into an animal's face.

Sausage

From this shape we can make arms and legs. It is simple to make by applying even pressure to the ball and continuing to roll, keeping it uniform thickness along its length.

For example:

The sausage shape when turned up at the end will form a foot, or can be marked to make a paw.

Cone

This shape is the basis for all bodies. It is made by rolling and narrowing the ball at one end, leaving it fatter at the other end.

For example:

The cone can be pulled out at the widest part to form the body of a bird.

Oval

This is the least used of the basic shapes, but is used to make cheeks, ears and other small parts. It is made in the same way as the sausage, by applying even pressure to the ball, but not taking it as far.

For example:

Smaller oval shapes can be used for animals' ears.

All four basic shapes were used to make this bear – a ball for his head, a cone for his body, a sausage for his legs and an oval for his muzzle. Five of the six tools shown opposite were used in his construction.

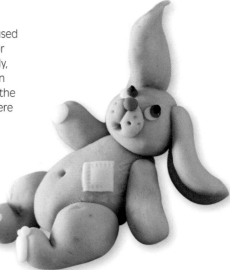

Constructing a Head

This step-by-step demonstration shows you how to make a female head bursting with life. She has lots of details in the construction of the face.

1 Start by rolling a ball into a pear shape. Add a small oval for the nose and attach to the centre of the face. Using tool no.11, indent the top and bottom of the mouth leaving a space in between. Join the edges at the sides (**A**).

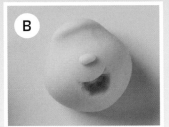

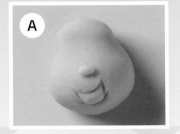

2 Hold the head in one hand and with the little finger of your other hand, indent the eye area by rocking the shape backwards and forwards a couple of times. Then, using the end of your paintbrush, push the centre of the mouth inside the head to make a cavity (**B**).

3 Roll a small banana shape for the teeth and place it under the top lip. Make two cone shapes in white for the eyeballs and attach just above and on either side of the nose. Add two small balls of dark blue sugarpaste to the top, and two smaller balls of black for the pupils. Roll two teardrop shapes for the ears and attach to either side of the head, keeping the top of each ear in line with the centre of the eyes. Indent the ears at the base with the end of your paintbrush (**C**).

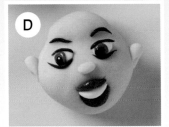

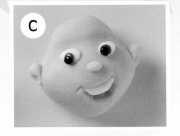

4 Roll two banana shapes in red sugarpaste for the lips and attach to the mouth. Outline the top and bottom of the eyes with a tiny lace of black sugarpaste and add the eyebrows in the same way (**D**).

5 Add the final details such as hair (see Hairstyles) and earrings, highlight the eyes with a dot of white edible paint on the end of a cocktail stick (toothpick) and dust the cheeks with pink dust food colour to give a healthy glow (**E**).

Tip
Experiment with the positioning of the eyes and eyebrows to give your characters different expressions.

A man's face has fewer details than a woman's but there are still key ways to add personality and character.

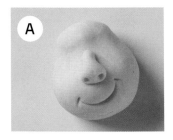

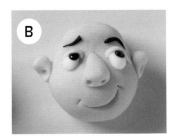

1 After rolling the head shape and indenting the eye area (see step 2 above), add a large cone shape for the nose. Mark the nostrils with tool no.5. Press the edge of a small circle cutter below the nose to mark the mouth. Add two small lines at either end of the mouth (**A**).

2 Roll two oval shapes in white for the eyes and attach on either side of the nose. Add a small black pupil to each eye. Add small banana shapes of flesh-coloured sugarpaste for the eyelids and add the eyebrows with a thin black lace. Make two cone shapes for the ears and attach to each side, indenting them with the end of your paintbrush (**B**).

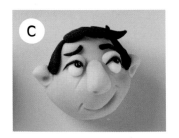

Tip
Use a flower former to hold the head in shape while you work on it.

3 For the hair, roll some flattened cones of black sugarpaste and secure into style on top of the head. For the final details, add a sliver of black to outline each eyelid, highlight the eyes with a dot of white edible paint on the end of a cocktail stick (toothpick) and dust the cheeks with pink dust food colour (**C**).

Using Head Shape to Add Personality

A crucial factor in imbuing your characters with personality is the shape of the head. The following examples show how using different head shapes can create a vast range of personas.

The square-shaped face implies a stocky person.

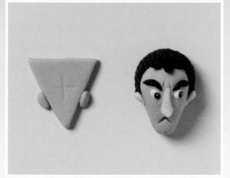

A person with a triangular face has pointed features and looks a bit shifty.

A rounded face signifies a happy personality.

This egg-shaped head would suit a studious person.

A hexagonal-shaped face indicates a bit of a thug.

The owner of this flat-shaped face would have a short, stocky body.

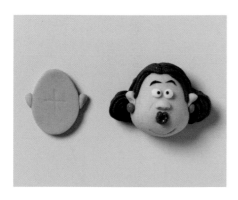

The pear-shaped face is the most comical and may be prone to having a double chin.

A heart-shaped face is very feminine and the hairline accentuates the shape.

An oval-shaped face is evenly balanced and is a very happy face.

Hairstyles

Hair is a great way of adding personality to your characters. For this example I will show you how to make a simple girl's hairstyle.

1 Fill the cup of a sugar press (or garlic press) with the desired colour of sugarpaste mixed with some white vegetable fat (shortening) and extrude the hair. Do not chop the hair off in a clump, but slide tool no.4 through a few strands, taking off a single layer at a time.

2 Apply edible glue around the head then starting at the back of the head, work around the sides adding thin layers of hair. If there is a parting at the back of the head, work from the parting to the side of the head, keeping in mind the direction in which you would comb the hair.

3 To make the bunches, extrude the hair and cut off several strands together, forming a bunch. Attach to the side of the head and shape as desired.

4 For the ringlets, take three strands of hair and twist them together, make three for each side of the head. Add a ribbon to finish by rolling a small white sausage shape.

Head and Body Shapes

As you can see from the image shown below, if a body has no neck, then the neck will be modelled with the head, and likewise, if the head has a neck, then the body will be modelled without one.

Basic cone-shaped body – the head has the neck.

Shaped body with neck and shoulders – the indented head has no neck.

Body made in two parts by rolling two cones in different colours. Cut both cones in half and attach the top of one to the base of the other. The head for this body has a neck.

Hands and Feet

When making an arm, first roll a sausage with rounded ends. Narrow the wrist area by rolling it gently then narrow just above the elbow. Make a diagonal cut at the top of the arm to fit the body shape. Flatten the hand end to look like a wooden spoon.

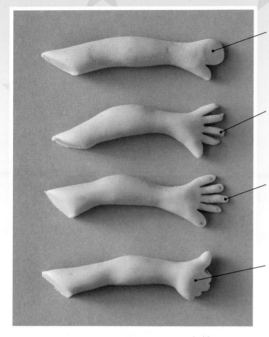

To make the hand, make a 'V' for the thumb and soften the edges with your finger.

Divide the rest of the hand into four fingers, keeping them an even width.

Roll each finger to soften the edges and mark the nails with dry spaghetti.

A less detailed hand with the fingers indented – use this when the hand does not require the fingers to be separate.

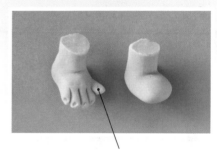

Cut out the toes as for the fingers only shorter.

Making Clothes

How you dress your characters is the final statement of their personality. Here I will show you how to make a pair of dungarees and a dress, both of which are very simple. With any clothing, you have to tailor it to the size of the body you are dressing, making sure the garments fit from side to side and from top to bottom.

Front of garment – trouser section and bib. Pockets with stitch marks add interest.

Back of garment – trouser section and braces. Patches add colour and fun.

Front of garment – square neck with a double frill and ribbon decoration.

Back of garment – high cut with a button opening. You could also add sleeves.

Shoes and Hats

Accessories such as hats and shoes are great fun to make. It is these little finishing touches that add to the charm of your finished character. Now you have lots of inspiration to create your own characters with bags of personality!

Girl's red shoe – with separate sole, strap, button detail and socks. Use dry spaghetti to attach directly to the end of the leg.

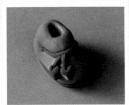

Pink slipper – with white bow. The inside of the shoe is hollowed out with tool no.1 for the leg to be slipped inside.

Blue boot – with red heart tie and sole. The top is hollowed out just wide enough to fit the leg.

Black and white sports shoe – with tongue, laces and stitch marked detail. Again, the inside of the shoe is hollowed out so that the leg can sit inside.

Bobble hat – formed from a cone of sugarpaste hollowed out with fingers to fit the head. Decorated with bands, stripes and furry bobbles extruded through a sugar press (or garlic press).

Cap – formed from a ball of sugarpaste, slightly flattened with a finger with a peak attached. Finished with a ball on the top and a contrasting trim around the peak.

Sun hat – made by mixing three or four different shades together to form a ball and flattening the top with a finger. A cut-out circle is attached for the brim.

Frilling

Frills can be used to decorate the side of the cake, or to make the edge of a pillow or a petticoat. You will need a special cutter called a Garrett frill cutter, which is available in two types – circle and straight. The circular cutter comes with three inner circles of different sizes to determine the depth of the frill. To make the frill, use a cocktail stick (toothpick), a frilling tool or the end of your paintbrush. Place your chosen tool on the edge of the frill and work it in a backwards and forwards motion, without putting too much pressure on it. The frill will lift where you have rolled. Continue with each section in turn until it is completed. A straight Garrett frill cutter will allow you to make a long frilled strip. The technique for frilling is exactly the same.

Circle cut with circle Garrett frill cutter, then frilled with a frilling tool.

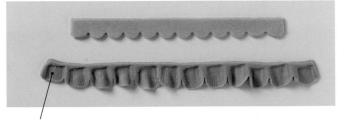

A strip of continuous frill, made with a straight Garret frill cutter and frilled with the end of a paintbrush.

Texturing Sugarpaste

A great way of adding interest to your cakes is to use textured patterns in the sugarpaste. Texture can be created using impression mats or with textured rolling pins. These can be used to add designs to a large area, such as a covered cake board, or for smaller details such as clothing. Some of the fantastic textures available are shown here.

Sunflowers Butterflies Stars Tulips Roses Fans

Bricks Basketweave Balloons Lattice Rice Pimples

Crimpers

Crimpers can be used in many different ways to decorate and enhance your work. Use them to trim around the edges of your cake boards or to decorate the sides of your cakes – you can make very interesting patterns with great ease. The crimpers shown here are plastic with a silicone ring, but you can also get metal ones. The plastic crimpers are non-stick, lightweight and come in a very handy see-through pack of ten assorted designs.

Place the crimpers over the sugarpaste and gently squeeze the sides together, applying enough pressure to indent the paste, then release. Make further indentations to follow where you left off. It may take a little practice to get the feel of them and not press too hard, but the results are very rewarding.

Crimpers are used to great effect on this mini cake, giving a wonderful decorative edge to the sugarpaste covering.

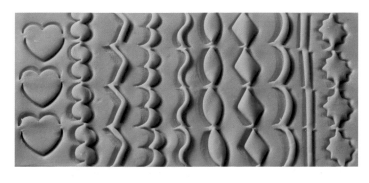

These are some of the pretty patterns you can achieve with crimpers.

Creating Animal Characters

Using the basic shapes as a starting point (see Basic Shapes), you can create a vast selection of different animals full of personality and charm. Each project gives detailed instructions for creating the featured characters, but here is a sample of some additional animals with advice on how to model them. Use these examples to practise and hone your modelling skills before you launch into the cake projects.

Mouse

Mice are well known for causing trouble and can be great characters to have on a cake. They come in many sizes and shapes, but all have shared characteristics. The shorter the nose the cuter the mouse will look; if it gets too long it will start to look more like a rat. Three basic shapes are needed: ball, cone and oval.

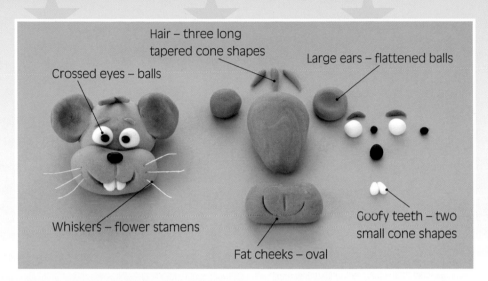

Crossed eyes – balls

Hair – three long tapered cone shapes

Large ears – flattened balls

Goofy teeth – two small cone shapes

Whiskers – flower stamens

Fat cheeks – oval

Monkey

This cheeky money is almost the same as the mouse, but we make him with balls of different sizes. His tuft of hair at the top makes him look really cute. He can be made using nine balls and two sausage shapes for the eyebrows.

Eyes and nose very close together

Small 'coconut' head

Big brow muscles

Small fat ears

Small mouth

Huge jaw

Lion

The lion is, of course, the King of the jungle, but my lion has such a sweet innocent look, he couldn't harm anyone. He is made from six balls, plus one large and one small cone shape.

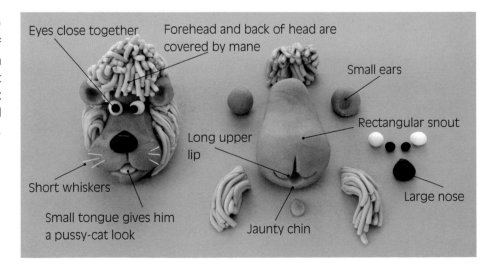

Eyes close together

Forehead and back of head are covered by mane

Small ears

Rectangular snout

Long upper lip

Short whiskers

Small tongue gives him a pussy-cat look

Jaunty chin

Large nose

Rabbit

This happy-go-lucky countryside resident is always ready for his next meal. He is full of character with his cross-eyed look and long ears. His eyes are close together and he has a distinctive goofy smile. He is made using eight cone shapes, five balls and four ovals.

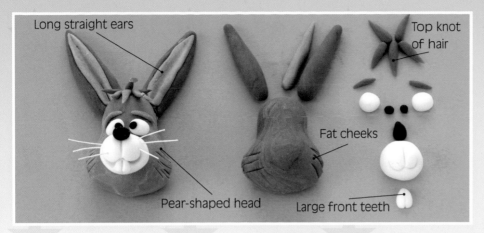

Long straight ears

Top knot of hair

Fat cheeks

Pear-shaped head

Large front teeth

Elephant

Every part of this huge animal is thick, fat and round. You could give him all sorts of expressions but this one is my favourite. The head is formed from a large cone, and then you pull out the trunk and continue to shape the face. The ears are made from oval shapes.

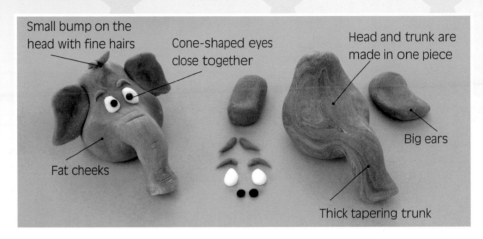

Small bump on the head with fine hairs

Cone-shaped eyes close together

Head and trunk are made in one piece

Big ears

Fat cheeks

Thick tapering trunk

Crow

What a classic cartoon character this bird is. The construction of the head is very simple, using three cone shapes, two circles and four balls, plus a few feathers.

Large overlapping eyes

Fine head feathers

Egg-shaped head

Cheek feathers

Hooked top beak overlapping the lower beak

Spindly neck

Cone-shaped beak

Dog

I couldn't complete a book without including my favourite Old English sheepdog. He never fails to enchant, with a simple tussled head that makes him irresistible. He is made using a cone shape for the head, flattened at the front, and simply covered in a sunburst of tapered cone shapes.

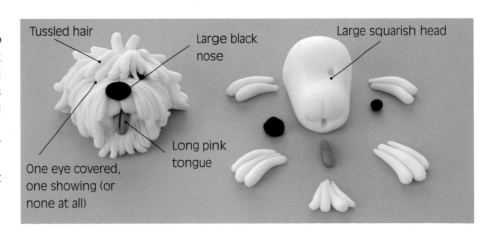

Tussled hair

Large black nose

Large squarish head

One eye covered, one showing (or none at all)

Long pink tongue

Recipes

Before you can get on with the business of decorating your cake, first you need to bake it! While there are thousands of books on cake making for you to refer to, here are my tried-and-tested recipes for both sponge and fruit cakes, for the small cakes that you will find at the end of every project, and for some additional things you will need to make.

Madeira Cake

This is a very nice firm cake that will keep for up to two weeks, giving you plenty of time to decorate it. It can also be frozen. I use it because it stays firm and will not sink when you place sugarpaste characters on the top. The recipe here is for a plain cake, but you can flavour both the sponge and the buttercream to suit your own taste.

Tip

The temperatures stated and baking times given are for fan-assisted ovens, which is what I use. If you are using a conventional oven, you will need to adjust the timings accordingly.

Ingredients

For a 20cm (8in) cake

- ★ 115g (4oz) plain (all-purpose) flour
- ★ 225g (8oz) self-raising (-rising) flour
- ★ 225g (8oz) butter (at room temperature)
- ★ 225g (8oz) caster (superfine) sugar
- ★ 4 eggs

Method

1 Preheat the oven to 160ºC (320ºF, Gas Mark 2–3). Grease the tin (pan) and line with greaseproof (wax) paper, then grease the paper as well.

2 Sift the flours into a large mixing bowl and add the butter and sugar. Beat together until the mixture is pale and smooth. Add the eggs and beat well, adding more flour if the mixture becomes too loose.

3 Spoon the mixture into the tin (pan), and then make a dip in the top with the back of a spoon to prevent the cake from rising too much.

4 Bake in the centre of the oven for 1–1¼ hours. Test the cake (see tip overleaf) and when it is cooked, remove it from the oven and leave it to stand in the tin (pan) for about five minutes, then turn it out onto a wire rack to cool fully.

5 Cover the cake around the sides and top with a coating of buttercream, then cover the cake with sugarpaste (see Covering Cakes).

Mini Cakes

These charming mini cakes are very popular and make the main cake go much further. Children love them, especially if they are made from sponge, which you can flavour to your taste. Ideally, use the Silverwood 6cm (2½in) mini pan set (see Suppliers), but if you don't have this you can just make one large cake and cut it into individual rounds using a 5cm (2in) round cutter. Serve on 7.5cm (3in) cake cards.

Ingredients

For 16 mini cakes or one 18cm (7in) cake to be cut into rounds

- ✱ 250g (8¾oz) self-raising (-rising) flour
- ✱ 250g (8¾oz) butter (at room temperature)
- ✱ 250g (8¾oz) caster (superfine) sugar
- ✱ 4 eggs

Method

1 Preheat the oven to 180ºC (350ºF, Gas Mark 4) and prepare the cake pans with silicone liners or with greaseproof (wax) paper.

2 Prepare the mixture as for the Madeira cake and half fill each cake pan. Bake in the centre of the oven for 15–20 minutes. You may wish to put a baking sheet on the bottom shelf to catch any drips. When cooked, remove from the oven and allow to cool to room temperature.

3 Leave the cooled cakes in the pans and slice neatly across the tops with a long-bladed knife, using the pan tops as a cutting guide.

4 Remove the pans from the base and gently pull the halves apart to remove the cakes. You may need to run a thin-bladed knife around the top edges to release any slight overspill. Place the cakes on a wire rack. Once cooled, keep them covered, as they will dry out very quickly.

5 Cover each mini cake around the sides and top with a coating of buttercream, then cover with sugarpaste (see Covering Cakes).

Rich Fruit Cake

This delicious cake improves with time, so always store it away before decorating it. I find it is generally at its best about four weeks after baking, provided it is stored properly and fed with a little extra brandy!

Tip

Test whether a cake is ready by inserting a fine skewer into the centre. If the cake is ready, the skewer will come out clean, if not, replace the cake for a few more minutes and then test it again.

Ingredients

For a 20cm (8in) cake

- ★ 575g (1lb 4¼oz) currants (small raisins)
- ★ 225g (8oz) sultanas (golden raisins)
- ★ 85g (3oz) glacé (candied) cherries
- ★ 85g (3oz) mixed (candied citrus) peel
- ★ 60ml (4tbsp) brandy
- ★ 285g (10oz) plain (all-purpose) flour
- ★ 2.5ml (½tsp) salt
- ★ 1.25ml (¼tsp) nutmeg
- ★ 3.75ml (¾tsp) mixed (apple pie) spice
- ★ 285g (10oz) soft (light) brown sugar
- ★ 285g (10oz) butter (at room temperature)
- ★ 5 eggs
- ★ 85g (3oz) chopped almonds
- ★ Grated zest of 1 orange and 1 lemon
- ★ 15ml (1tbsp) black treacle (blackstrap molasses)

Method

1 Place all the fruit and peel into a bowl and mix in the brandy. Cover the bowl with a cloth and leave to soak for 24 hours.

2 Preheat the oven to 140°C (275°F, Gas Mark 1). Grease the tin (pan) and line with greaseproof (wax) paper, then grease the paper as well.

3 Sieve the flour, salt and spices into a mixing bowl. In a separate bowl, cream the butter and sugar together until the mixture is light and fluffy.

4 Beat the eggs and then add a little at a time to the creamed butter and sugar, beating well after each addition. If the mixture looks as though it is going to curdle, add a little flour.

5 When all the eggs have been added, fold in the flour and spices. Then stir in the soaked fruit and peel, the chopped almonds, treacle (molasses) and the grated orange and lemon zest.

6 Spoon the mixture into the prepared tin (pan) and spread it out evenly with the back of a spoon.

7 Tie some cardboard or brown paper around the outside of the tin (pan) to prevent the cake from overcooking on the outside before the inside is done, then cover the top with a double thickness of greaseproof (wax) paper with a small hole in the centre to let any steam escape.

8 Bake the cake on the lower shelf of the oven for 4¼–4¾ hours. Do not look at the cake until at least 4 hours have passed, then test it (see tip).

9 When cooked, remove from the oven and allow to cool in the tin (pan). When quite cold, remove from the tin (pan) but leave the greaseproof (wax) paper on as this helps to keep the cake moist. Turn the cake upside down and wrap it in more greaseproof (wax) paper, then loosely in polythene and store in an airtight container. Store in a cool, dry place.

10 You can feed the cake with brandy during the storage time. To do this, make a few holes in the surface of the cake with a fine skewer and sprinkle a few drops of brandy onto the surface. Reseal and store as above. Do not do this too often though or you will make the cake soggy.

11 Glaze the cake with apricot glaze (see Essential Purchases), then cover it with a layer of marzipan and sugarpaste (see Covering Cakes).

Carrot Cake

This is a very old recipe imported from America where it is sometimes called Passion Cake. It is a very sweet cake and carrots lend texture and wonderful moistness. The cream cheese frosting gives it a much-needed sharpness and is used in place of buttercream.

Ingredients

For a 20cm (8in) cake

* 125g (4½oz) butter (at room temperature)
* 125g (4½oz) soft (light) brown sugar
* 125g (4½oz) honey
* 250g (8¾oz) self-raising (-rising) flour
* 10ml (2tsp) cinnamon
* 250g (8¾oz) grated carrot
* Juice of 1 lemon

For the frosting

* 30g (1oz) butter (at room temperature)
* 50g (1¾oz) cream cheese
* 125g (4½oz) icing (confectioners') sugar
* Juice of 1 lemon

Method

1 Preheat the oven to 180°C (350°F, Gas Mark 4). Grease the tin (pan) and line with greaseproof (wax) paper, then grease the paper as well.

2 Cream the butter and sugar until pale and fluffy, then stir in the honey.

3 Sift in the flour and cinnamon, and add the carrots. Fold and mix well adding the lemon juice to loosen the mixture, and then turn into the tin (pan).

4 Bake for 1 hour, checking the cake by inserting a skewer into the centre – if done it will come out clean.

5 For the frosting, beat the butter and cream cheese together then fold in the sugar and add the lemon juice.

6 Coat the cake around the sides and top with frosting, then cover with sugarpaste (see Covering Cakes).

Tip
This cake should be nice and moist, so don't overcook it.

Almond and Cherry Cake

This lovely light fruit loaf slices beautifully to reveal the glacé (candied) cherries.

Ingredients

For a 20cm (8in) loaf

* ☆ 100g (3½oz) butter (at room temperature)
* ☆ 125g (4½oz) caster (superfine) sugar
* ☆ 3 large (US extra large) eggs
* ☆ 50g (1¾oz) ground almonds
* ☆ 125g (4½oz) self-raising (-raising) flour
* ☆ 100g (3½oz) glacé (candied) cherries
* ☆ 50g (1¾oz) sultanas (golden raisins)

Method

1 Preheat the oven to 150ºC (300ºF, Gas Mark 3). Grease the loaf tin (pan) and line with greaseproof (wax) paper, then grease the paper as well.

2 Beat the butter and sugar together until pale and fluffy, then add the eggs one at a time.

3 Fold in the almonds and the flour, and then the fruit. You can leave the cherries whole or halve them.

4 Pour the mixture into the tin (pan) and bake for 1½ hours. Allow the cake to cool completely in the tin before turning it out.

5 Cover the cake around the sides and top with a coating of buttercream, then cover with sugarpaste (see Covering Cakes).

Tip

Do not open the oven door for at least an hour at the start of the baking time, otherwise the mixture will sink in the middle.

Edible Glue

This is the glue that holds sugarpaste pieces together, used in every project in this book. Always make sure your glue is edible before applying it to your cake.

Ingredients

- ★ 1.25ml (¼tsp) CMC (Tylose) powder
- ★ 30ml (2tbsp) boiled water, still warm
- ★ A few drops of white vinegar

Method

1 Mix the CMC (Tylose) powder with the warm boiled water and leave it to stand until the powder has fully dissolved. The glue should be smooth and to a dropping consistency. If the glue thickens after a few days, add a few more drops of warm water.

2 To prevent contamination or mould, add a few drops of white vinegar.

3 Store the glue in an airtight container in the fridge and use within one week.

Tip

To make a stronger edible glue, add an extra pinch of CMC (Tylose) to the basic recipe and mix into a stiff paste.

Buttercream

A generous coating of buttercream precedes the covering of sugarpaste on all sponge cakes. The classic version is flavoured with a few drops of vanilla extract, but you could substitute this for cocoa powder (unsweetened cocoa) or grated lemon/orange zest to suit your particular taste.

Sweet and delicious, buttercream is simple to make and is the ideal covering for both large and mini sponge cakes. Smooth on a generous layer with a palette knife before they are covered in sugarpaste.

Ingredients

To make 480g (1lb) of buttercream

- ★ 110g (4oz) butter (at room temperature)
- ★ 30ml (2tbsp) milk
- ★ 350g (12oz) sifted icing (confectioners') sugar

Method

1 Place the butter into a mixing bowl and add the milk and any flavouring required.

2 Sift the icing (confectioners') sugar into the bowl a little at a time. Beat after each addition until all the sugar has been incorporated. The buttercream should be light and creamy in texture.

3 Store in an airtight container for no more than one week.

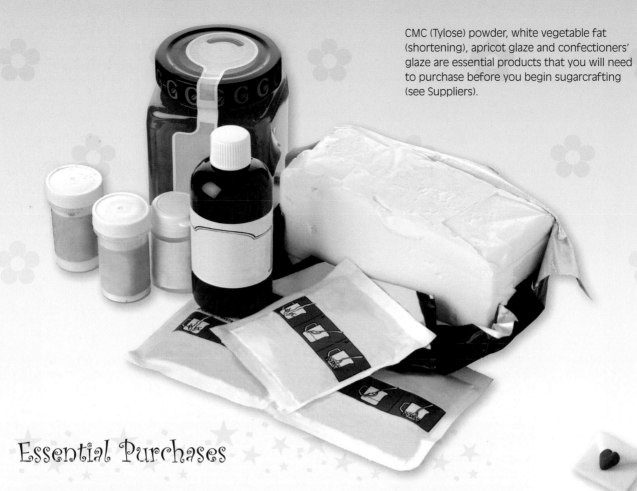

CMC (Tylose) powder, white vegetable fat (shortening), apricot glaze and confectioners' glaze are essential products that you will need to purchase before you begin sugarcrafting (see Suppliers).

Essential Purchases

A visit to your local cake-decorating or sugarcraft shop is a must – not only can you buy all the necessary products there, you will also come away very inspired! These products cannot be made at home with any great ease, and therefore need to be purchased.

✿ White vegetable fat (shortening)
This is used for softening sugarpaste so that it can be extruded through a sugar press (or garlic press) more easily to make hair, grass, fluff etc. If you find your sugarpaste has dried out a bit, knead in a little of this to make it soft and pliable again.

✿ CMC (Tylose) powder
Carboxymethylcellulose is a synthetic and inexpensive thickening agent that is used to convert sugarpaste into modelling paste (see Sugarpaste for Modelling), and also used for edible glue.

✿ Apricot glaze
This glaze is painted onto fruit cakes before adding a layer of marzipan (see Covering a Cake with Marzipan). It is made from apricot jam, water and lemon juice, which is boiled then sieved. Although it would be possible to make your own, I don't know anyone who does, as it is so easy to use straight from the jar.

✿ Confectioners' glaze
This product is used to highlight the eyes, shoes or anything you want to shine on your models. It is particularly useful if you want to photograph your cake, as it will really add sparkle. Apply a thin coat and let it dry, then apply a second and even a third coat to give a really deep shine. It is best kept in a small bottle with brush on the lid – this way the brush is submerged in the glaze and doesn't go hard. If you use your paintbrush to apply it, then you will have to clean it with special glaze cleaner.

Abbreviations and Equivalents

g = grams

oz = ounces (1oz = 30g approx)

cm = centimetres (1cm = ⅜in approx)

mm = millimetres

in = inches (1in = 2.5cm approx)

ml = millilitres

tsp = teaspoon (1tsp = 5ml)

tbsp = tablespoon (1tbsp = 15ml)

fl oz = fluid ounces

Cup Measurements

If you prefer to use cup measurements, please use the following conversions. (Note: 1 Australian tbsp = 20ml)

Liquid

½ cup = 120ml (4fl oz)

1 cup = 240ml (8fl oz)

Butter

1tbsp = 15g (½oz)

2tbsp = 25g (1oz)

½ cup/1 stick = 115g (4oz)

1 cup/2 sticks = 225g (8oz)

Caster (superfine) sugar

½ cup = 100g (3½oz)

1 cup = 200g (7oz)

Icing (confectioners')sugar

1 cup = 115g (4oz)

UK / US Terms

UK	US
black treacle	blackstrap molasses
bicarbonate of soda	baking soda
cake tin	cake pan
caster sugar	superfine sugar
cling film	plastic wrap
CMC powder	Tylose powder
cocktail stick	toothpick
cocoa powder	unsweetened cocoa
cornflour	cornstarch
currants	small raisins
glacé cherries	candied cherries
greaseproof paper	wax paper
icing sugar	confectioners' sugar
mixed peel	candied citrus peel
mixed spice	apple pie spice
plain flour	all-purpose flour
self-raising flour	self-rising flour
soft brown sugar	light brown sugar
sugarpaste	rolled fondant icing
sultanas	golden raisins
white vegetable fat	shortening

Covering Cakes

Most beginners can successfully cover a cake with sugarpaste. However, a professional finish – a glossy surface free of cracks and air bubbles with smooth rounded corners – will only result from practice.

1 Prepare the cake with a layer of buttercream (see Recipes) or apricot glaze and marzipan depending on whether it is a sponge or a fruit cake.

2 Take sufficient sugarpaste to cover the complete cake. The quantity required for each of the cakes in this book is given at the start of each project. Work the paste until it is quite soft and smooth, then place it onto a surface lightly dusted with icing (confectioners') sugar.

3 Roll out the paste with a non-stick rolling pin – spacing rods can be used to maintain a uniform thickness (**A**). The depth of the paste should be approximately 5mm (⅛in). As you roll the paste, move it regularly to ensure it has not stuck to the surface.

4 Measure the cake by taking a measuring tape up one side, over the top and down the other side. The sugarpaste should be rolled out in the shape of the cake to be covered (round for a round cake, square for a square cake and so on), and rolled out a little larger than the measurement just made.

A

Tip

When covering a cake, try to do it in natural daylight, as artificial light makes it more difficult to see flaws. Sometimes imperfections can be covered, but sometimes they will occur where you are not going to put decorations so you need to strive for a perfect finish every time. However, if things don't go to plan, don't worry; the sugarpaste can be removed and re-applied.

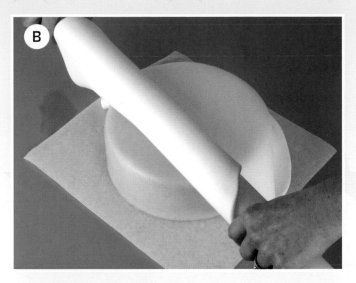

5 Lift and drape the paste over the cake using a rolling pin (**B**). Carefully lift the sides of the paste, brushing the top surface of the cake in one direction to eliminate any air trapped in between. Continue to smooth the top with the palm of your hand and then use a smoother (**C**).

6 For the sides, lift, flatten and rearrange any folds at the bottom removing any creases. Do not smooth downwards as this may cause a tear at the top edge. With your hand, ease the sugarpaste inwards at the base and smooth the sides with an inward motion using your hand and a smoother.

7 Trim the bottom edge with a marzipan knife (**D**). Trim the paste in stages as the icing shrinks back.

8 Check the surface and sides for any flaws and re-smooth if necessary. For air bubbles, insert a pin or fine needle into the bubble at an angle and gently rub the air out, then re-smooth to remove the tiny hole.

9 Once you are happy with the surface, use either the smoother or the palm of your hand and polish the top of the cake to create a glossy finish.

10 Ideally the covered cake should be left to dry out for 24–48 hours at room temperature before decorating.

Tip

Keep the dusting of icing (confectioners') sugar on the work surface very light; too much will dry out the paste and make it crack.

Covering the Cake Board

Moisten the board with cooled boiled water, then roll out the specified quantity of sugarpaste to an even thickness, ideally using spacing rods (see General Equipment). Cover the board completely with sugarpaste using the same method as covering the cake, smoothing the paste out and trimming the edges neatly with a marzipan knife. Some paste can then be saved by removing a circle from the centre of the board, which will be covered by the cake. For a professional finish edge the board with ribbon, securing it with non-toxic glue.

> ### Tip
> An alternative method for covering a board involves placing the cake on to the board prior to covering them, then using a single piece of sugarpaste to cover them both. The sugarpaste needs to be rolled out much larger for this method.

Covering the cake board in sugarpaste gives your cakes a really professional appearance and allows you to add extra decorations and embellishments. As a finishing touch, edge the board with a length of ribbon.

Covering a Cake with Marzipan

A layer of marzipan is used on fruit cakes only. Sponge cakes should be covered with buttercream (see Recipes) prior to covering with sugarpaste. For fruit cakes, coat first with apricot glaze (see Essential Purchases) as this will help the marzipan to stick. The quantity of marzipan required will depend on the size of the cake, but as a general guide, half the weight of the cake will give you the correct weight of marzipan.

1 Place the glazed cake onto a sheet of greaseproof (wax) paper. Place the marzipan between spacing rods and roll to an even thickness large enough to cover the cake.

2 Lift the marzipan onto the rolling pin and place it over the cake. Push the marzipan into the sides of the cake using a cupped hand to ensure there are no air pockets.

3 Trim off any excess marzipan with a knife and then run cake smoothers along the sides and the top of the cake until they are straight.

4 Leave the marzipan to dry for one or two days in a cool temperature.

5 Before applying the sugarpaste, sterilize the surface of the cake by brushing the marzipan with a clear spirit such as gin, vodka or kirsch. Ensure the entire surface is moist; if there are any dry areas the paste will not stick to the marzipan and could result in air bubbles.

> ### Tip
> If you are using marzipan, make sure nobody eating the cake is allergic to nuts. This is very important as nut allergies are serious and can have fatal consequences.

Dowelling Cakes

A stacked cake is dowelled to avoid the possibility of the upper tiers sinking into the lower tiers. The 'Let It Snow' cake is the only cake that requires dowelling but you could use this technique to add extra tiers to any of the other cakes, if you want to adapt the designs.

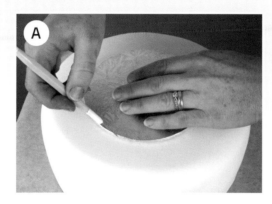

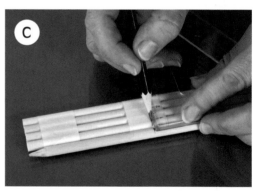

1 Place a cake board the same size as the tier above in the centre of the bottom tier cake. Scribe around the edge of the board (**A**) leaving an outline then remove the board.

2 Insert a wooden dowel vertically into the cake 2.5cm (1in) from the outline, down to the cake board below. Take a pencil and mark the dowel level with the surface of the cake (**B**) and then remove the dowel. Repeat with the other dowels required (four is usually sufficient).

3 Tape the dowels together and draw a line across using the highest mark as a guide (**C**). You can then saw across all the dowels to make them exactly the same length. Alternatively, you can unwrap the marked dowels and cut each of them separately with a pair of pliers or strong kitchen scissors.

4 Place the cut dowel back into the hole, then arrange the other dowels into the three, six and nine o'clock positions to the first one (**D**). Ensure that all the inserted dowels are level and have flat tops.

5 The cake board of the upper tier should rest on the dowels and not on the cake. The very slight gap in between the cake and the board of the upper tier will not be noticed and is normally covered by decoration.

Have Your Cake and Eat It!

You may well have cooked up a storm and made the perfect party cake, but how do you get your creation from kitchen to guest without a hitch? Storing the cake ahead of the event is the first consideration, then, if the party is not at your home, transporting it to the venue in one piece is of primary importance. Finally, some top tips follow on cutting the cake and removing items before eating it.

Cake Boxes

The most essential item for safe storage and transportation of your cake is a strong box designed for the job. You can buy special boxes for stacked cakes (see Suppliers) that open up at the front to enable the cake to slide inside. The front then closes and finally the lid is placed on the top. Make sure the box is deep and high enough to take the cake without damaging it when the lid goes on. To make the cake even safer inside the box, you can buy non-slip matting from most DIY stores. A piece of this cut to size and placed under the cake board will prevent it moving around inside the box.

Tip

Keep your cakes away from direct sunlight at all times, as bright light will fade the sugarpaste.

Room Temperature

The temperature of the room the cake is stored in is crucial to its condition. If your house or the party venue is very humid it can be disastrous. You would do well to invest in a portable dehumidifier to keep the moisture at bay, especially during wet weather. Never think that your figures will benefit from leaving a heater on in the room; you will find that they become too warm and soft and will flop over.

Transportation

If you are transporting a cake, you need to be sure that the boot (trunk) of the car is high enough when closed, and the cake itself is made secure on a flat surface for the journey. Never put the cake on the back seat of the car, as this is not a level surface and the cake could be ruined when you apply the brakes. Remember too that if the vehicle gets too hot, it will affect the cake. It can melt buttercream and make sugarpaste soft.

Cutting the Cake

Many people have no idea how to begin to cut a cake. If it is not cut properly it could end up in a pile of crumbs. The number of portions you require will have some bearing on the way you cut the cake. A simple way is to mark points on the edge of the cake at the desired intervals. Use a sharp serrated knife to cut across the cake and then downwards keeping the blade of the knife clean at all times. Then cut the section into smaller pieces.

The Decorations

If you wish to keep the decorations or figures on the cake, remove them before cutting. If they are to be stored, then do not put them into a plastic container, as they will sweat. Place them inside a clean cardboard box wrapped in tissue paper. Your decorations and figures will keep for a long time if you make sure they are kept in a dry atmosphere. Should you wish to display them, the best place is inside a glass-fronted cabinet where they will be safe.

Any decorations with wires attached should never be inserted directly into the cake as the metal can cause contamination. Instead, insert a cake pick, pushing it right into the cake until the top is level with the surface, then place the wires inside. Alternatively, you can make a mound of sugarpaste to insert wires into, and this can be hidden with more decoration.

When making figures for your cake, never insert cocktail sticks (toothpicks), always use pieces of dry raw spaghetti. Remove these before eating the figures. Children will always want to eat the figures, no matter how long it has taken you to make them.

Tip
If you wish to add candles to decorate your cake, always insert the candle holder into the cake first. When the candles are lit, they will prevent any wax from spilling on to the cake. Remove them before cutting the cake.

Frequently Asked Questions

Q: What if the road I am taking to deliver the cake is very bumpy?
A: Place the cake on a flat surface in the car. If necessary place a foam mat under the box and drive slowly!

Q: Is the foot well of the car the best place to transport a cake?
A: It is a good place, but make sure that there is nothing on the seat to slide off on to the cake – with disastrous consequences.

Q: What if it is a really hot day when the cake is delivered?
A: Keep the air conditioning on if you have it.

Q: If the cake is too heavy for me to lift at my destination what should I do?
A: Never try to lift a large cake on your own; ask if there is a truck available, or even a small table on wheels to place it on.

Q: Where is the cake best displayed?
A: Try to display the cake in a tidy, uncluttered area that will not detract from the design.

Q: What should I look for once the cake has been assembled?
A: Check that the ribbon around the board is still lined up correctly and has not become loose or dislodged. Make sure your cake topper is securely fixed and perfectly upright.

Q: What shall I do if I make a mark on the cake while I am transporting it to its destination?
A: Always carry a fixing kit with you, which should include edible glue, a little royal icing in a piping (pastry) bag, and a few spare decorations you can apply to cover the mark, depending on the design of the cake.

The Projects

Rock 'n' Roll

King of DIY

Domestic Bliss

Father's Day

Let It Snow

Whole Nine Yards

Hobby-Mad Minis

Rock 'n' Roll

This rockin' Teddy boy's got the sound, the looks and all the moves to knock his girl right off her feet. With plenty of fifties fun, a sprinkle of razzle dazzle and a good pinch of nostalgia, this classic design will have any man dusting down his blue suede shoes and reaching for the drainpipe trousers!

"With my velvet voice I'm gonna rock your world, uh huh huh!"

You will need

Sugarpaste

* ★ 675g (1lb 7¾oz) red
* ★ 515g (1lb 2oz) dark blue
* ★ 515g (1lb 2oz) white
* ★ 315g (11¼oz) black
* ★ 140g (5oz) pale yellow
* ★ 110g (3⅞oz) flesh
* ★ 38g (1½oz) light brown
* ★ 27g (1oz) lime green
* ★ 20g (¾oz) grey
* ★ 20g (¾oz) dark brown
* ★ 2g (⅛oz) fuchsia
* ★ 2g (⅛oz) jade

Materials

* ★ 30cm (12in) star-shaped cake
* ★ Cornflour (cornstarch)
* ★ White vegetable fat (shortening)
* ★ Confectioners' glaze
* ★ Edible glue (see Recipes)
* ★ Dry spaghetti
* ★ Rainbow Dusts: jewel fire red, jewel light gold, starlight laser lemon, pastel pink, metallic ginger glow

Equipment

* ★ 33cm (13in) hexagonal cake drum
* ★ Round cutters: 6cm (2⅜in), 5cm (2in), 4cm (1½in), 3cm (1¼in), 2.5cm (1in), 2cm (¾in), 1.5cm (½in), 1cm (⅜in), 5mm (⅛in)
* ★ Black ribbon 15mm (½in) wide x 1m (40in) long
* ★ Non-toxic glue
* ★ Basic tool kit (see General Equipment)

Covering the cake and board

1 To cover the board roll out 600g (1lb 5oz) of red sugarpaste to an even 3mm (⅛in) thickness. Cover the board in the usual way (see Covering the Cake Board). Save any leftover sugarpaste to use for the decoration. Edge the board with the black ribbon, securing it with non-toxic glue.

2 To cover the cake roll out 500g (1lb 1½oz) of dark blue sugarpaste to a 5mm (⅛in) thickness. Prepare the cake and cover the top of the cake only, trimming the edges around the top of the star.

3 To cover the sides of the cake roll out 400g (14oz) of white sugarpaste into a strip measuring 7 x 120cm (2¾ x 47¼in). Lightly dust the strip with cornflour (cornstarch), then loosely roll it up. Attach the end of the sugarpaste to the edge of the cake and carefully unroll it around the sides, securing it as you go.

Tip
If you find it too difficult to work with one piece to cover the side of the cake, do it in sections instead.

4 Add three spotlights to the top of the cake by rolling out 40g (1½oz) of pale yellow sugarpaste, and cut out a 6cm (2⅜in), a 5cm (2in) and a 4cm (1½in) circle. Secure to the top of the cake, dust the spotlights with jewel light gold dust and add a light scattering over the top of the cake.

The musical decorations

1 For the records roll out 50g (1¾oz) of black sugarpaste and cut out three 3cm (1¼in) circles and three 2.5cm (1in) circles. To mark the grooves, indent the larger circles with 2.5cm (1in), 2cm (¾in) and 1.5cm (½in) round cutters, and indent the smaller circles with 2cm (¾in), 1.5cm (½in) and 1cm (⅜in) round cutters (**A**).

2 To make the labels roll out 3g (⅛oz) of pale yellow sugarpaste and cut out six 1cm (⅜in) circles. Attach one to the centre of each record, push a hole through the centre with tool no.5 (**A**) and dust with jewel light gold dust.

3 To make the notes thinly roll out the black sugarpaste left over from the records, and use a 1cm (⅜in) circle and fine strips of black to complete the various notes (**A**). Arrange the notes and the records around the front half of the cake. Give the decorations two coats of confectioners' glaze, allowing one coat to dry before applying the second.

The acoustic guitar

1 For the guitar body roll 28g (1oz) of light brown sugarpaste into an oval shape measuring 7 x 4cm (2¾ x 1½in) and pinch in the centre to make into a figure-eight shape. Flatten with your fingers to a depth of 8mm (¼in). Take a 1.5cm (½in) round cutter and mark the sound hole in the centre of the guitar. Indent the top of the body with the end of a paintbrush to make a hollow for the neck to fit inside (**B**).

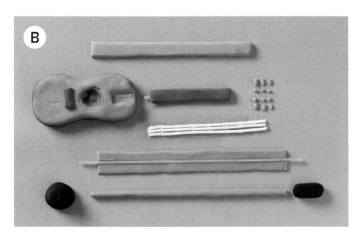

2 To make the neck roll out 6g (¼oz) of dark brown sugarpaste and cut out a strip measuring 8 x 1cm (3⅛in x ⅜in). Cut off 5mm (⅛in) and use this to form the bridge, securing it below the sound hole. Push a length of dry spaghetti down through the centre of the neck to give it support and secure it firmly to the end of the body (**B**). Flatten the top end of the neck to widen it slightly.

3 For the strings soften 10g (⅜oz) of pale yellow sugarpaste with white vegetable fat (shortening) and fill the cup of a sugar press (or garlic press). Extrude lengths of paste and lay three along the neck of the guitar from the bridge, to within 1cm (⅜in) from the top. Mark lines across the strings with tool no.4 (**B**).

4 For the tuning pegs take 1g (⅛oz) of light brown sugarpaste and make six tiny balls and six tiny cones. Attach the six balls to the flattened end of the neck and attach three cones down each side (**B**). Place the guitar on the cake.

5 Make the guitar strap by rolling out 5g (¼oz) of light brown sugarpaste. Cut a strip measuring 16 x 1cm (6¼ x ⅜in) and attach to the guitar (**B**). Give the guitar body two coats of confectioners' glaze to make it shine.

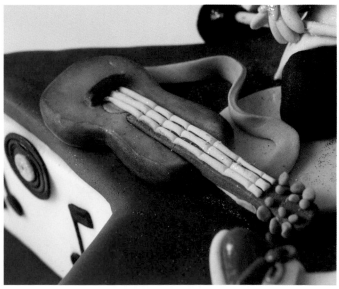

The microphone

1 For the stand roll 10g (⅜oz) of grey sugarpaste into a strip measuring 15 x 1cm (6 x ⅜in). Run a line of edible glue along the centre and place a piece of dry spaghetti on top. Fold the strip around the spaghetti and roll it into a smooth round shape. Trim off any excess paste.

2 For the microphone roll 2g (⅛oz) of black sugarpaste into a small sausage shape, slip this over the top of the stand and prick it all over with tool no.5.

3 For the base roll 5g (¼oz) of black sugarpaste into a cone shape. Flatten and insert the stand into the centre. Set aside to harden. Apply confectioners' glaze to the black parts of the stand and microphone.

The Teddy boy

1 For the blue suede shoes equally divide 14g (½oz) of dark blue sugarpaste and roll into two balls, and then into rectangular prisms. For the soles, equally divide 7g (¼oz) of black sugarpaste and roll into two sausage shapes. Flatten with your finger and attach to the shoes (**C**).

2 Using tool no.4, mark vertical ridges around the soles and indent the heels across the back. Mark the front of each shoe with two vertical lines at the front. Mark a semicircle on the top of each shoe using the edge of a 2cm (¾in) round cutter, and then indent a vertical line down the centre for the opening of each shoe. Still using tool no.4, mark the laces across the line (**C**).

3 For the socks roll 5g (¼oz) of white sugarpaste, into a sausage shape and divide equally. Attach to the top of each shoe (**C**) and push a piece of dry spaghetti down through the centre, leaving 3cm (1¼in) showing. Give the soles two coats of confectioners' glaze and set the shoes aside.

Tip
Make the body and legs together for extra support, and keep the body upright so it doesn't lose height.

4 For the drainpipe trousers roll 100g (3½oz) of black sugarpaste into a ball, then into a carrot shape. Place on to the work surface with the thickest end at the bottom and slightly flatten and smooth the top of the shape with your hand. Using tool no.4, push the point into the centre of the shape and divide into two at the thickest end. With the flat of your fingers, remove the edges to form two round legs, making them slightly longer as you do so (**C**).

5 Place the figure on a cake card. Bend the right leg at the knee, taking the foot to the back. The left leg is slightly bent at the knee but stretched out in front. Push a piece of dry spaghetti through the body and into the right knee. Attach the shoes to the end of the legs, securing with edible glue.

6 For the shirtfront roll out 10g (⅜oz) of white sugarpaste and cut out a rectangle measuring 5 x 3cm (2 x 1¼in). Attach to the front of the body from the neck to the waistline. Make the collar by rolling out the remaining white sugarpaste into a strip 8cm (3⅛in) long, making a diagonal cut at each end to shape (**C**). Place the collar around the spaghetti at the neck, leaving enough room in the centre for the neck.

Tip
Place the head inside a flower former while you work on it to keep the rounded shape.

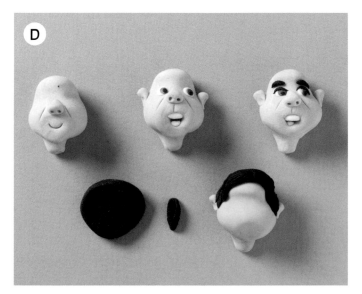

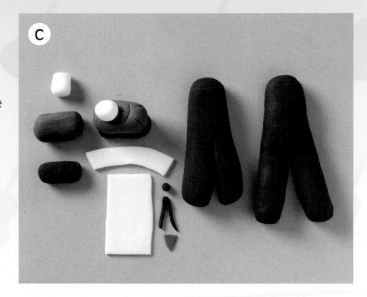

7 For the bootlace tie roll a thin lace of black sugarpaste and attach to the shirtfront. Cut out a small triangle of red sugarpaste for the toggle and secure to the top of the tie (**C**). Dust the toggle with jewel fire red dust.

8 For the head roll 30g (1oz) of flesh-coloured sugarpaste into a ball then pull down the neck and indent the eye area (see Constructing a Head). Make a straight cut at the neck (**D**) and use the offcuts for the nose and ears.

9 For the nose make a small cone shape and attach in the centre of the face, pinching the end of the nose to turn it up slightly. Using tool no.5, mark the nostrils at the base of the cone (**D**).

10 For the mouth mark a smile using tool no.11, then push the end of your paintbrush into the mouth to open it wide, pulling down the bottom. Take a small amount of white sugarpaste and roll into a banana shape for the top teeth, and a smaller one for the bottom teeth, making sure the teeth have a space between them. With the rounded end of tool no.4, mark lines on the face on either side of the nose (**D**).

11 For the eyes add two small white balls on either side of the nose. Use smaller balls of dark brown sugarpaste for the irises, directing the eyes to the left, and on top of these add two tiny black balls for pupils. Add a small banana shape of black sugarpaste over each eye, then a thicker one for the eyebrows (**D**).

12 For the ears roll two small cones of flesh-coloured sugarpaste and attach to each side of the head, indenting with the end of your paintbrush (**D**).

13 For the hair roll 9g (⅜oz) of black sugarpaste into a ball then hollow it out with your fingers to form a round cap. Place this over the head, pulling it forwards to frame the face. Using tool no.4, mark lines on the hair, bringing down sideburns in front of the ears. To make the flick at the front, roll a small black sausage and curl it around the handle of your paintbrush, marking the hair with lines using tool no.4 (**D**). Attach to the front of the hair, bringing it down over the forehead.

14 Slip the completed head over the spaghetti at the neck, turning it to the left. Apply some confectioners' glaze to the eyes and hair.

15 For the jacket roll out 35g (1¼oz) of pale yellow sugarpaste and cut out a rectangle measuring 10 x 8cm (4 x 3⅛in), curving the top corners to round off the lapels (**E**). Attach to the back of the body and bring around to the front, leaving the edges loose and turning over the lapels.

Tip
You may have to adjust the shape and size of the jacket to fit your figure.

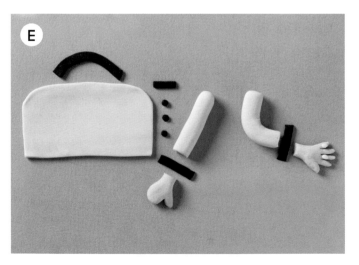

E

16 For the arms roll another 35g (1¼oz) of pale yellow sugarpaste into a sausage shape and divide with a straight cut, leaving two rounded ends for the tops of the sleeves (**E**). Push a short piece of dry spaghetti into each shoulder, bend the right arm at the elbow and secure the arm to the spaghetti at the shoulder. Attach the left arm in the same way and rest it on the left knee. Push a short piece of dry spaghetti into each wrist.

17 Position the figure on top of the cake and secure with edible glue. Place the microphone across the knees.

18 For the hands take 8g (¼oz) of flesh-coloured sugarpaste, equally divide and roll into two cones then flatten the hands and model the thumb and fingers (see Hands and Feet). Slip the hands over the spaghetti at the wrist. Roll a small ball and oval shape for the rings and attach to the fingers (**E**). Dust the rings with jewel light gold dust.

19 For the collar, cuffs, pocket top and buttons roll out 10g (⅜oz) of black sugarpaste into a long narrow strip. Cut off 7cm (2¾in) for the collar, make a diagonal cut at each end and arrange around the jacket lapels. Cut two pieces for cuffs and one for the pocket top and attach with edible glue. Attach three small black balls to the front of the jacket (**E**) and mark the corresponding buttonholes with tool no.4. Dust the jacket with starlight laser lemon dust.

The Teddy girl ·

1 For the body roll 45g (1½oz) of white sugarpaste into a cone shape. Turn the cone around so that the widest part is at the top. Squeeze the paste into a ridge across the chest then divide it into two with your finger. Begin to round off the breasts until you have an even shape on both sides (**F**). Place the body on top of the cake and push a piece of dry spaghetti down through the centre, leaving 2cm (¾in) showing at the top. Push a short piece of dry spaghetti into the shoulders.

2 For the legs roll 28g (1oz) of flesh-coloured sugarpaste into a sausage shape. Make a diagonal cut in the centre and indent the knee area at the back of both legs (**F**). Attach the right leg at the hip and keep some height under the knee area, supporting the leg with a piece of foam until it dries. Attach the left leg, placing the knee over the edge of the cake. Push a short piece of dry spaghetti into each ankle.

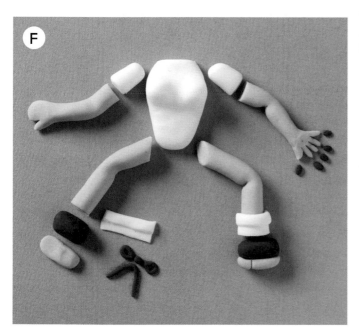

3 For the shoes equally divide 8g (¼oz) of red sugarpaste and roll into two small sausage shapes. Make the soles using 4g (⅛oz) of light brown sugarpaste equally divided and rolled into two sausage shapes. Attach the soles to the shoes and flatten with your finger, marking the heel lines across with tool no.4 (**F**). Slip the shoes over the spaghetti at the base of the legs.

4 For the socks roll 3g (⅛oz) of white sugarpaste into a strip measuring 2 x 6cm (¾ x 2⅜in). Turn over the top of the strip and cut in half to make two socks. Place over the join between the shoes and the legs. Make a small bow for each shoe by rolling a thin lace of red sugarpaste. Cut off a short length for the tail and attach to the shoe. Make two small loops and place them together, finishing with a small ball in the centre (**F**).

5 For the sleeves roll 7g (¼oz) of white sugarpaste into a sausage shape 4cm (1½in) long. Cut in half and attach over the spaghetti at the shoulders (**F**). Push a short piece of spaghetti into the bottom of each sleeve.

6 For the arms roll 14g (½oz) of flesh-coloured sugarpaste into a sausage shape, cut in half with a straight cut and bend each arm at the elbow. Make the hands as for the Teddy boy. Take 1g (⅛oz) of red sugarpaste to make the nails, rolling ten small oval shapes and attach to the fingers of each hand (**F**). Position the arms as shown, supporting them with foam if necessary until dry.

7 For the collar roll out 5g (¼oz) of white sugarpaste to a measurement of 2 x 7cm (¾ x 2¾in). Make a diagonal cut at each end, and fold the piece over into a soft fold (**G**). Attach around the neckline, leaving room for the head.

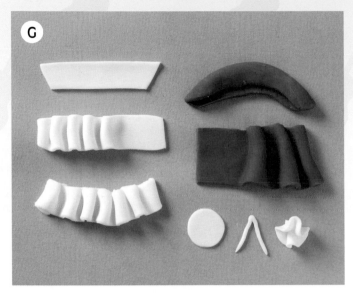

8 For the petticoats roll out 23g (¾oz) of white sugarpaste and cut into two strips measuring 12 x 20cm (4¾ x 8in). Frill both pieces (see Frilling) and secure the top edge, leaving the lower edge very loose (**G**). Apply some edible glue above the knee and to the side and attach the first frill, placing the second frill over the top.

9 For the back of the skirt roll out 25g (⅞oz) of red sugarpaste into an oval shape measuring 5 x 12cm (2 x 5in). Turn over the top to make a soft edge (**G**). Place the piece on the back of the figure, bringing the edges around to the top of the leg.

10 For the front of the skirt roll out 20g (¾oz) of red sugarpaste into a rectangle measuring 5 x 15cm (2 x 6in). Make some soft folds, being very careful not to crack them, and attach to the front and side of the body, lifting the edges to give them movement (**G**). Save any leftover red sugarpaste for the lips and accessories.

11 For the corsage roll a thin lace of white sugarpaste and attach to the side of the skirt. Roll out 2g (⅛oz) of white sugarpaste and cut out a 2cm (¾in) circle, pinching it in at the centre to form a flower (**G**). Secure onto the lace.

12 For the head roll 30g (1oz) of flesh-coloured sugarpaste into a ball, and then pull down the neck. Pinch out the cheeks and pull down the chin with your thumb. Cut off the neck and use the offcuts for the nose and ears. Roll a small cone shape for the nose and attach to the centre of the face, marking nostrils with tool no.5. Add a beauty spot with a dot of black (**H**).

13 For the mouth mark a smile with the large end of tool no.11 and open the mouth area with the end of your paintbrush. Add the teeth as for the Teddy boy, and roll two small banana shapes in red for the lips. Using tool no.4, mark lines on either side of the nose (**H**).

14 For the eyes add two small balls of white and attach on either side of the nose. Add two tiny balls of dark blue sugarpaste for the irises, and add two smaller balls of black for the pupils. The eyes should be looking to the right. Outline the top of each eye with a thin lace of black sugarpaste (**H**).

15 For the earrings roll out 1g (⅛oz) of red sugarpaste and cut out two 1cm (⅜in) circles. Take out the centre of the each circle with a 5mm (⅛in) round cutter and attach the resulting hoops to the ears (**H**).

Tip
Refer to Constructing a Head for more advice on modelling facial features.

16 For the hair soften 17g (½oz) of pale yellow sugarpaste with white vegetable fat (shortening) and fill the cup of a sugar press (or garlic press). Extrude the hair and attach it to the back and side of the head, keeping the strands short and working from the base to the crown.

17 For the fringe lay out a thin row of the strands of hair and take out the edge of the layer with a 3cm (1¼in) round cutter to make a half moon shape (**H**). Pull the top of the hair together and attach around the top of the face.

18 For the ponytail refill the press and extrude much longer strands of hair. Take off about six strands and twist them together to make a ringlet (see Hairstyles). Attach to the back of the head. Finish off with a small band of red to go over the top (**H**). Dust the cheeks with pastel pink dust and coat the nails, lips and eyes with confectioners' glaze.

Tip
It is very important that you keep the height of the body, and that the waist is defined.

The jukebox ·

1 For the cabinet roll 130g (4½oz) of black sugarpaste into a sausage shape then roll out to a thickness of 1.5cm (½in) measuring 10 x 6cm (4 x 2⅜in). Keeping the top rounded, make a straight cut at the base (**I**).

2 For the speakers roll out 12g (½oz) of dark brown sugarpaste, cut out a 4cm (1½in) circle and cut in half. Attach to the top half of the cabinet. Cut out a strip for the rectangular speakers measuring 8 x 1.5cm (3⅛ x ½in) and cut in two. Using tool no.4, mark with a crisscross pattern. Attach to the lower part of the cabinet, leaving room for the three lights to go down the centre. Dust the speakers with metallic ginger glow dust. Soften 10g (⅜oz) of white sugarpaste with white vegetable fat (shortening) and fill the cup of a sugar press (or garlic press). Extrude long strands and edge the speakers with single strands (**I**).

3 For the control panel roll out 2g (⅛oz) of white sugarpaste into a thin strip measuring 3cm x 8mm (1¼ x ¼in). From 1g (⅛oz) of red sugarpaste, roll out a small rectangle and attach in the centre. Add small balls of black sugarpaste to either side for the knobs (**I**).

4 To make the three coloured lights you will need 2g (⅛oz) each of lime green, fuchsia and jade sugarpaste. Cut out a 1.5cm (½in) circle in each colour and position evenly in between the speakers. From 1g (⅛oz) of black sugarpaste, cut out three 5mm (⅛in) circles and attach to the centre of each light (**I**).

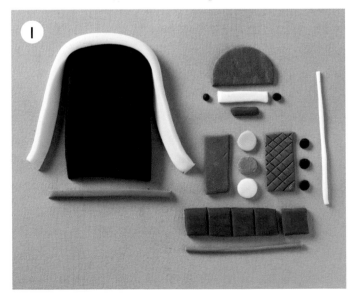

5 For the fluorescent light roll 25g (⅞oz) of lime green sugarpaste into a sausage shape 25cm (10in) long. Take a cutting wheel (or pizza cutter) and cut the sausage in half lengthways, so you have one straight edge and one rounded edge. Attach one strip to the outside of the cabinet (**I**).

6 To make the red lights, roll out 18g (¾oz) of red sugarpaste to a 5mm (⅛in) thickness and cut a strip measuring 2.5 x 8cm (1 x 3⅛in). Divide the piece into five sections (**I**) and attach two to the bottom, two to the middle and one at the top of the fluorescent light border.

7 Edge the lights with 3g (⅛oz) of grey sugarpaste rolled into a thin lace, cut into short lengths and attach to the top and bottom of the lights. Edge the base of the cabinet by rolling 6g (¼oz) of grey sugarpaste into a strip measuring 5mm x 12cm (⅛ x 4¾in) (**I**).

8 Push two lengths of dry spaghetti into the base of the jukebox, leaving 4cm (1½in) showing at the base. Push into the back of the cake and support if necessary until dry.

A Little More Fun!

Rock Cakes

These matching mini cakes, baked in Silverwood 7.5cm (3in) round mini cake pans, continue the rock 'n' roll theme with musical notes, records, coloured lights and the guitar and blue suede shoes from the main cake. They also feature bright shades of jade, fuchsia, red, yellow and lime green sugarpaste for a truly vibrant look – a perfect party pick-me-up!

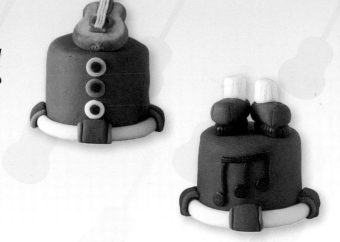

King of DIY

The wallpaper's falling down and he's just sawn a hole through the worktop, but you daren't comment or criticize ... after all, he means well! If you have your own DIY-obsessed man sorting out your problems at home, this comical cake reflects just what you are thinking, and he is sure to see the funny side, right?

"I should have known this would be another DIY disaster!"

You will need

Sugarpaste

* 600g (1lb 5oz) pale blue
* 535g (1lb 3oz) grey
* 155g (5½oz) dark blue
* 110g (3⅞oz) white
* 80g (2⅞oz) yellow
* 76g (2½oz) light brown
* 56g (2oz) flesh
* 26g (⅞oz) dark brown
* 25g (⅞oz) red
* 3g (⅛oz) black

Materials

* 15cm (6in) square cake
* Confectioners' glaze
* Edible glue (see Recipes)
* Dry spaghetti
* White edible paint
* Liquid food colours: red, dark brown and old gold
* Rainbow Dust: starlight silver saturn

Equipment

* 28cm (11in) square cake drum
* Textured rolling pin (optional)
* Square cutters: 2.5cm (1in), 2cm (¾in)
* Round cutters: 3cm (1¼in), 2cm (¾in), 1cm (⅜in)
* FMM wood impression mat
* Pale blue ribbon 15mm (½in) wide x 60cm (24in) long
* Non-toxic glue
* Basic tool kit (see General Equipment)

Covering the cake and board

1 To cover the board roll out 470g (1lb ½oz) of grey sugarpaste to an even 5mm (⅛in) thickness. If desired, roll a textured rolling pin over the top, thinning the paste to 3mm (⅛in). Cover the board in the usual way (see Covering the Cake Board). Edge the board with the pale blue ribbon, securing it with non-toxic glue.

> ## Tip
> Renshaw's grey shade of ready-made sugarpaste is great as it saves having to mix black and white to make grey.

2 To cover the cake roll out 600g (1lb 5oz) of pale blue sugarpaste to an even 5mm (⅛in) thickness. Prepare the cake and cover it in the usual way (see Covering Cakes), making sure you secure each corner and the top edges first to prevent the paste stretching. Attach the cake to the centre of the board using edible glue mixed with sugarpaste to make a stiff paste.

The DIY man

1 For the lower body and legs roll 70g (2½oz) of dark blue sugarpaste into a ball then roll the legs out from either side, leaving the paste bulky in the centre. Bend the left leg at the knee area and keep the right leg straight (**A**). Push 3cm (1¼in) of dry spaghetti into the end of each leg.

King of DIY

2 For the boots equally divide 34g (1⅛oz) of light brown sugarpaste, roll two short fat sausage shapes and turn up one end of each to form the foot, keeping the toe very rounded. Make the soles using 2g (⅛oz) of dark brown sugarpaste equally divided. Roll into two sausage shapes then flatten each foot area, shaping to fit the bottom of the boots (**A**). Mark the heels across with tool no.4. Slip the boots over the spaghetti at the end of each leg.

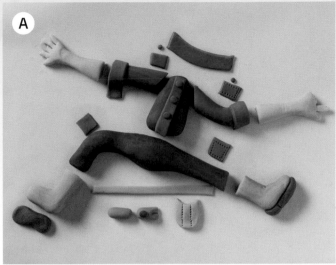

3 Place the lower body onto the side of the cake, allowing the right foot to stand on the board, and the left foot on the top of the cake. Push a piece of dry spaghetti into the centre of the lower body and into the cake to secure.

4 For the upper body take 45g (1½oz) of dark blue sugarpaste and roll into a cone shape (**A**). Place the cone in the centre and on top of the lower body then push a piece of dry spaghetti down through the middle of the cone and into the lower body, leaving 2cm (¾in) showing at the top. Push 1cm (⅜in) of dry spaghetti into each shoulder.

5 For the front of the overalls roll out 1g (⅛oz) of dark blue sugarpaste and cut out a strip measuring 5cm x 5mm (2 x ⅛in). Attach to the front of the body. Use the leftover paste to make three small buttons, rolling small balls then flattening them with your finger. Attach to the strip with edible glue (**A**).

6 For the knee-patches and shoulder trims roll out 2g (⅛oz) of dark blue sugarpaste, cut out four 2cm (¾in) squares and stitch mark around the edges using tool no.12. Attach one patch on each knee and one trim on each shoulder. Add a tiny button of dark blue sugarpaste to the centre of the shoulder trims (**A**).

7 For the belt roll out 3g (⅛oz) of light brown sugarpaste into a strip measuring 1 x 10cm (⅜ x 4in). Attach around the waist, crossing over at the front. Make a small pouch by rolling 1g (⅛oz) of light brown sugarpaste into an oval shape and flatten with your finger. Make a curve at the top of the shape with the edge of a 2cm (¾in) round cutter. Using tool no.12, stitch mark two horizontal lines down the pouch (**A**).

8 For the claw hammer roll 1g (⅛oz) of grey sugarpaste into a small sausage shape. Flatten the back of the shape and make the other end straight. Using tool no.4, mark a line in the centre front of the hammer to make the claw. Add a small dot of red to the top (**A**) then attach to the top of the pouch.

9 For the sleeves roll 30g (1oz) of dark blue sugarpaste into a sausage shape. Make a diagonal cut in the centre and a straight cut at each end of the sleeve. Keep the left sleeve straight and bend the right sleeve at the elbow (**A**). Push a short piece of dry spaghetti into the end of each sleeve ready to attach the lower arm. Set the leftover paste aside to make the cuffs.

10 For the arms and hands equally divide 26g (1oz) of flesh-coloured sugarpaste. Roll into two sausage shapes and model the hands (see Hands and Feet). Keep the index finger on the right hand straight and curl under the remaining fingers (**A**). Make a straight cut at the elbow and slip over the spaghetti at the end of the sleeve. Attach the completed left arm to the spaghetti at the shoulder and place the hand on top of the cake.

11 To make the cuffs roll out the leftover dark blue sugarpaste and cut two strips measuring 1 x 3cm (⅜ x 1¼in). Place them over the join of each arm and sleeve (**A**).

12 For the head roll 30g (1oz) of flesh-coloured sugarpaste into a smooth ball and pull down the neck area by twisting the paste between your finger and thumb (**B**). Trim the neck and use the offcuts for the nose and ears.

13 Pinch the chin to pull it down then roll a small cone shape for the nose and attach this in the centre of the face. Mark the nostrils with tool no.5 and add a line to either side of the nose and mouth using tool no.4. Mark the mouth with tool no.11 then straighten out the top lip using the blade of tool no.4. Open the mouth with the soft end of your paintbrush. For the teeth, roll two small banana shapes of white sugarpaste and place at the top and bottom of the mouth. Mark two vertical lines over the nose (**B**).

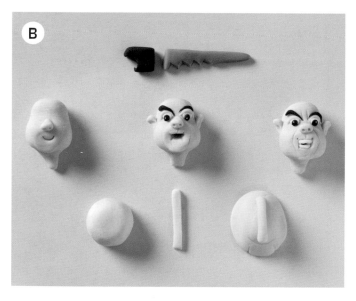

14 For the eyes roll two small balls of white sugarpaste and place on either side of the nose, flattening with your finger. Roll two smaller balls of dark brown sugarpaste for the irises and attach over the whites. Add two smaller balls of black sugarpaste for the pupils. Roll two small banana shapes of leftover flesh-coloured sugarpaste for the eyelids and place over each eye. Attach two small banana shapes of dark brown sugarpaste for the eyebrows. Highlight the eyes with a dot of white edible paint on the end of a cocktail stick (toothpick) (**B**).

15 For the ears use two small teardrop shapes of leftover flesh-coloured sugarpaste. Attach to either side of the head and indent with the end of your paintbrush (**B**).

16 For the hard hat roll 13g (½oz) of yellow sugarpaste into a ball then hollow out the centre with the rounded end of tool no.3 until it fits the top of the head. Pull out the edges to form the rim of the hat. Mark two lines at the centre front of the hat. Roll a further 1g (⅛oz) of yellow sugarpaste into a sausage shape and flatten with your finger then place over the top of the hat (**B**). Mark the centre front of the hat with the edge of a 1cm (⅜in) round cutter then attach the hat to the top of the head.

17 Slip the completed head over the spaghetti at the neck. For the collar, roll out 3g (⅛oz) of dark blue sugarpaste and cut a strip measuring 1 x 8cm (⅜ x 3⅛in). Make a diagonal cut at both ends and attach around the neckline (**A**).

Tip
Place the head into a flower former to keep its shape while you work on the facial expression.

King of DIY

The saw

1 For the blade roll 10g (⅜oz) of grey sugarpaste into a sausage shape and flatten to a 5mm (⅛in) thickness by 1.5cm (½in) wide by 4cm (1½in) long. Make a straight edge at the top using tool no.4 and shape the blade to a point, then make a diagonal cut at the tip of the blade so that it will rest on top of the cake. Using tool no.4, cut out the teeth making small 'V' shapes along the blade (**B**). Push a length of dry spaghetti down through the blade to keep it straight, leaving 1cm (⅜in) showing at the top to take the handle. Set the blade aside on a flat surface.

2 For the handle shape 4g (⅛oz) of dark brown sugarpaste into a rectangle measuring 1.5 x 2cm (½ x ¾in). Take out a semicircle at the top of the handle using a 1cm (⅜in) round cutter (**B**). Slip the handle over the dry spaghetti on the blade and secure with edible glue. Attach the saw into the man's right hand securely, placing the end of the blade on the cake. This arm may need some support with foam until it has dried.

The toolbox

1 To make the base of the box roll out 20g (¾oz) of yellow sugarpaste into a rectangle 1cm (⅜in) thick, measuring 2 x 5cm (¾ x 2in) (**C**).

2 For the sides roll out 44g (1½oz) of yellow sugarpaste to a 5mm (⅛in) thickness, cutting out two shapes for the back and front of the box measuring 3 x 5.5cm (1¼ x 2⅛in), and two shapes for the ends measuring 3 x 2cm (1¼ x ¾in) (**C**). Place the base of the box onto a flat surface, then attach the front, back and ends together with edible glue.

3 Make two rope handles by rolling 1g (⅛oz) of grey sugarpaste into a very thin lace. Cut in half and twist the two together to make a rope 6cm (2⅜in) long and divide equally (**C**). Attach one rope handle to each end of the box. Set aside until the box has hardened off.

C

The tools

1 For the spanner roll 4g (⅛oz) of grey sugarpaste into a sausage shape 5cm (2in) long. Flatten each end with your finger and use tool no.11 to shape each end (**D**).

2 For the set square roll out 4g (⅛oz) of grey sugarpaste and cut out a 2.5cm (1in) square. Take out a 2cm (¾in) square from the corner to form the shape (**D**).

3 For the screwdriver roll 2g (⅛oz) of grey sugarpaste into a sausage shape. Press the end to flatten slightly then pinch into a point at the end. Make a straight cut at the end and push a piece of dry spaghetti through the centre, leaving 2cm (¾in) showing. For the handle, roll 1g (⅛oz) of dark blue sugarpaste into a sausage shape, cut a straight edge at the top and slip over the spaghetti (**D**).

4 For the claw hammer roll 3g (⅛oz) of grey sugarpaste into a sausage shape. Mark a vertical line at one end using tool no.4. Turn up the marked end to shape the tool and make a straight cut at the other end. Push a short length of dry spaghetti into the centre, leaving 2cm (¾in) showing. For the handle, roll 1g (⅛oz) of dark brown sugarpaste into a sausage shape. Make a straight cut at one end and slip over the spaghetti (**D**). Dust the grey parts of the tools with starlight silver saturn dust.

5 For the flask roll 4g (⅛oz) of red sugarpaste into a thick sausage shape. Make a straight cut at one end. Form the top by rolling 2g (⅛oz) of black sugarpaste into a short sausage shape and make a straight cut at one end. Push a piece of dry spaghetti through the centre of the flask, leaving 1cm (⅜in) showing at the top. Slip the black top over the spaghetti and add a small handle by rolling a thin lace curved into a loop (**D**). Attach with edible glue. Place the tools and flask inside the toolbox and position on the cake.

6 For the screws take 1g (⅛oz) of grey sugarpaste, divide equally and roll into two small cone shapes. Flatten the tops and make the opposite ends very sharp and pointed (**D**). Attach to the cake in front of the toolbox.

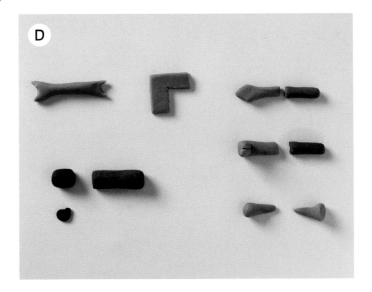

D

The gloves

For the gloves equally divide 12g (½oz) of grey sugarpaste and roll into two balls then into cone shapes. Flatten the wide end of each cone with your finger. On each glove, mark the thumb with tool no.4 and remove the edges until smooth. Divide the rest of the fingers into four, and round each one off until they are smooth. Mark the cuffs with tool no.4 (**E**) and place the gloves on the cake behind the man.

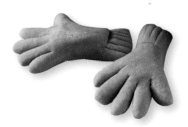

The tape measure

1 For the tape holder roll 9g (⅜oz) of dark brown sugarpaste into a ball and flatten slightly with your finger. Take a 2cm (¾in) round cutter and indent the top. Roll a small rectangle of grey sugarpaste, folding it over loosely to make a clip, and attach to the top of the holder (**E**).

2 For the tape roll out 3g (⅛oz) of white sugarpaste and cut a strip measuring 10cm x 5mm (4 x ⅛in). Secure the tape to the holder (**E**) and attach to the top of the cake.

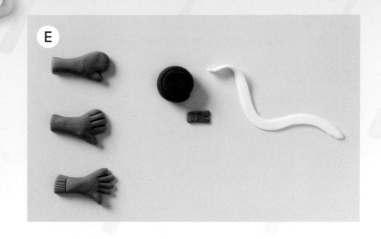

The planks of wood

For the planks mix together 20g (¾oz) of white sugarpaste with 20g (¾oz) of light brown to make a pale brown shade. Roll out the paste to a measurement of 12 x 5cm (4¾ x 2in). Place the wood impression mat over the top to mark the wood design. Cut into two pieces (**F**) and attach to the board at the side of the cake. Highlight the wood grain with a little dark brown liquid food colour.

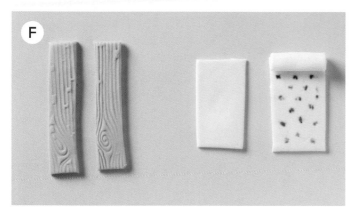

The wallpaper

For the sheets of wallpaper roll out 40g (1½oz) of white sugarpaste into a strip measuring 23 x 4.5cm (9 x 1¾in). Cut one length to measure 13cm (5in), roll up at the top and attach to the corner of the cake. Attach the second piece of wallpaper but only apply the glue halfway up, keeping the top part loose to drape over the dog. Paint a spotty pattern onto the wallpaper with red liquid food colour (**F**).

The dog

1 For the body mix 40g (1½oz) of white sugarpaste with 14g (½oz) of light brown to make a pale brown shade. Take off 20g (¾oz) and roll into a small cone shape (**G**). Push a length of dry spaghetti down through the centre, leaving 1cm (⅜in) showing at the top.

2 For the back legs take off 9g (⅜oz) and divide equally, then roll into two balls. Narrow the balls with your finger to lengthen the shapes and attach to the back of the dog (**G**).

3 For the front legs take off 8g (¼oz) and roll into a sausage shape, turning up the foot at each end. Cut in half and turn each leg over on to its side, then slice off the bulk from the back. Secure the legs to the front of the body and indent all four paws with the rounded end of tool no.4 (**G**).

4 For the head roll 13g (½oz) into a ball, indent the top and slip over the spaghetti. Take off enough paste to make a small cone for the lower jaw, flatten with your finger and attach under the front of the head, leaving enough room for the tongue. Roll a small ball of black sugarpaste to make the nose and attach to the head (**G**).

Tip
Model the dog on a small cake card and place him on the cake when he is complete.

5 For the ears equally divide 2g (⅛oz) of the paste and roll into two small cone shapes, flatten with your finger and attach the narrow ends to each side of the head (**G**).

6 To make the tail roll 2g (⅛oz) into a tapered cone shape, make a diagonal cut at the thickest end and attach to the back of the dog (**G**).

7 Roll a small cone shape of red sugarpaste for the tongue and insert into the mouth, marking down the centre with tool no.4. Add some splodges of red sugarpaste to the paws to look like paint. Paint some markings on the dog using brown liquid food colour (**G**). Place the dog in front of the wallpaper and drape the loose piece over his face.

King of DIY

The crooked picture

1 For the picture roll out 5g (¼oz) of white sugarpaste into a 3cm (1¼in) square and indent the centre with a 2cm (¾in) square cutter, or use tool no.4 to mark (**H**). Paint the frame with old gold liquid food colour and outline it with brown liquid food colour and a fine paintbrush. Then use this to paint the picture in the frame (**H**).

2 For the hanger take 1g (⅛oz) of yellow sugarpaste and take off enough to roll a thin lace. Secure the lace to the back of the picture, and then roll the remainder of the yellow paste into a ball and attach this to the back of the picture to allow it to hang proud of the cake (**H**). Push a short piece of dry spaghetti into the cake and make a nail using a small amount of grey sugarpaste. Push the nail over the spaghetti and flatten the end. Apply some edible glue to the ball behind the picture and secure it to the cake.

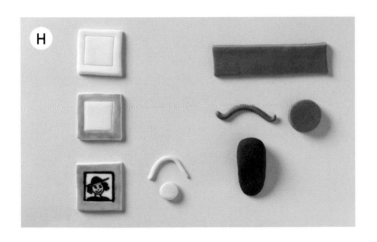

Tip
Make sure that the weight of the picture is taken by the ball, not the lace, as this will snap under strain.

The paint pot and paintbrush

1 For the paint pot roll out 27g (1oz) of grey sugarpaste to a 5mm (⅛in) thickness and cut out a 3cm (1¼in) circle for the base. Cut a strip measuring 2.5 x 4.5cm (1 x 1¾in) for the side (**H**). Apply some edible glue around the side of the base and attach the strip, making a neat join.

2 For the paint roll 15g (½oz) of red sugarpaste into a fat cone shape. Keeping the pot upright, push the thickest end into the pot and flatten the other end to lengthen it. Place the pot on its side and position it on the corner of the cake board. Roll a small grey lace for the handle and secure to either side of the pot (**H**).

3 For the paintbrush roll 9g (⅜oz) of dark brown sugarpaste into a ball and make it into a wooden spoon shape for the handle, making a straight cut at the widest part. For the bristles, roll out 4g (⅛oz) of light brown sugarpaste into a fat rectangle shape and attach to the end of the straight edge. Mark the bristles with tool no.4. Cut out a 2cm (¾in) circle of grey sugarpaste, cutting off one-third to make a straight edge and attach to the brush handle (**I**).

4 For the paint on the brush roll 2g (⅛oz) of red sugarpaste into a rectangle and attach to the bristles with edible glue (**I**). Secure the brush beside the paint pot on the board, adding a few tiny balls of red sugarpaste for drips. Highlight any parts of the cake that you want to shine with two coats of confectioners' glaze.

Tip
Allow the first coat of confectioners' glaze to dry before applying the second coat.

A Little More Fun!

Builders' Bites

These coordinating mini cakes are baked in Silverwood 7.5cm (3in) round mini cake pans, using the sponge cake recipe that is supplied with the tins. The saw, planks, hard hat and paintbrush are all modelled in the same way as on the main cake but any of the tools could be used instead. And after all that sawing and painting, a nice cup of tea and one of these cakes will be just what the worker needs!

Domestic Bliss

Is your man a multi-tasking domestic god? If so, he deserves a big thank you on his birthday. So for one day of the year let him forget the washing up, put down the duster and leave the laundry unfolded. Tell him to put his feet up and relax on the sofa while enjoying a large slice of this amusing and wonderfully true-to-life cake creation.

"Don't worry! I've got everything under control ... more or less."

You will need

Sugarpaste

* 825g (1lb 13oz) white
* 212g (7½oz) cream
* 160g (5⅝oz) flesh
* 123g (4½oz) light brown
* 90g (3¼oz) dark blue
* 88g (3oz) yellow
* 85g (3oz) lime green
* 76g (2⅝oz) light blue
* 55g (2oz) grey
* 50g (1¾oz) dark brown
* 34g (1⅛oz) red
* 30g (1oz) jade
* 22g (¾oz) pink
* 17g (½oz) baby blue
* 13g (½oz) black
* 10g (⅜oz) green
* 6g (¼oz) pale yellow

Materials

* 18 x 8cm (7 x 3in) cake
* White vegetable fat
  (shortening)
* Confectioners' glaze
* Edible glue (see Recipes)
* Dry spaghetti
* Rainbow Dust: plain
  and simple pink

Equipment

* 30 x 15cm (12 x 10in)
  oval cake drum
* Round cutters: 3cm (1¼in),
  2.5cm (1in), 2cm (¾in),
  1.5cm (½in)
* Straight-edged crimper
* Bronze ribbon 15mm (½in)
  wide x 1m (40in) long
* Non-toxic glue
* Basic tool kit (see
  General Equipment)

Covering the board and cake ....

1 To cover the board you will need 100g (3½oz) of white, 100g (3½oz) of cream, 100g (3½oz) of light brown, 50g (1¾oz) of grey and 50g (1¾oz) of dark brown sugarpaste. Roll each colour into small balls and knead them together, making sure you do not over mix. Roll into a smooth ball and roll out (**A**) to cover the board in the usual way (see Covering the Cake Board). Edge the board with the bronze ribbon, securing it with non-toxic glue.

2 To cover the cake first take out a 5 x 6cm (2 x 2⅜in) x 1.5cm (½in) deep piece from the top to form the sink. Prepare the cake then roll out 600g (1lb 5oz) of white sugarpaste to an even 5mm (⅛in) thickness. Gently press the paste into the sink area and arrange over the sides. Indent the lines on the draining board while the paste is still soft.

3 To make the drawer and cupboard fronts roll out 90g (3¼oz) of cream sugarpaste and cut out two drawer fronts measuring 2.5 x 5.5cm (1 x 2⅛in) and two cupboard fronts measuring 5 x 6.5cm (2 x 2½in). Mark a line around the fronts using the rounded end of tool no.4 (**B**). Attach to the front of the cake.

4 Make the handles by rolling out 1g (⅛oz) of black sugarpaste, cut into four 1.5cm (½in) lengths and attach one to the front of each cupboard and drawer (**B**). Attach the cake towards the back of the covered cake board, using edible glue mixed with sugarpaste to make a stiff paste.

The taps (fawcet)

1 For the spout roll 1g (⅛oz) of grey sugarpaste into a sausage shape 4cm (1½in) long. Push a piece of dry spaghetti into the centre back of the sink and slip two-thirds of the sausage over the top, bending the top over to form the shape of the spout. Roll a small ball and flatten it, pressing it underneath the spout (**B**).

2 For the taps (fawcet) roll a further 1g (⅛oz) of grey sugarpaste into two small sausage shapes and push a piece of dry spaghetti down the centre of each. Insert one end of the spaghetti into each side of the spout at an angle. Roll four small cone shapes for the tap handles and attach to the top of the sausage shape. Add a small ball of white in the centre to complete (**B**).

The towel rail and towels

1 For the rail roll out 2g (⅛oz) of grey sugarpaste into a strip measuring 1 x 6cm (⅜ x 2⅜in). Run a line of edible glue down the centre and place a piece of dry spaghetti over the top. Fold over the paste and trim off the excess with tool no.4 (**C**). Roll the piece into a smooth shape and cut off any spaghetti that is showing at the ends. Attach the rail to the left-hand side of the cake.

2 **For the two tea towels** thinly roll out 25g (⅞oz) of red sugarpaste. Cut out one rectangle measuring 8 x 6cm (3⅛ x 2⅜in) and one measuring 5.5 x 4.5cm (2⅛ x 1¾in). Make the stripes by thinly rolling out 3g (⅛oz) of white sugarpaste. Cut four strips and lay two on one end of each towel. Gently roll over the strips with your rolling pin to flatten them slightly and trim the excess at the sides (**C**). Attach the larger towel over the rail and the smaller one over the top of the left-hand drawer.

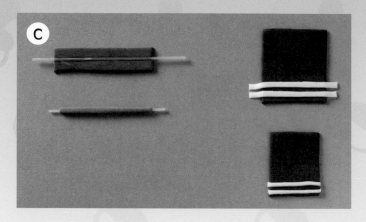

The dark blue crockery

1 **For the teapot** roll 11g (⅜oz) of dark blue sugarpaste into a ball. Roll out another 2g (⅛oz), cut out a 2cm (¾in) circle to make the lid and attach to the top of the ball. Roll a small ball from the leftover paste and attach to the top of the lid (**D**).

2 **Make the spout** by rolling 1g (⅛oz) of dark blue sugarpaste into a short sausage shape, curve the spout and attach to the teapot. Push a hole in the end of the spout with the pointed end of tool no.3. Roll a thin lace of dark blue sugarpaste and curve into the shape of the handle. Secure to the side of the pot (**D**).

3 **For the jug** roll 6g (¼oz) of dark blue sugarpaste into a fat sausage shape and pinch out the lip with your fingers. Turn the jug upside down, roll a thin lace for the handle and secure to the side of the jug (**D**).

4 **For the cup** roll 3g (⅛oz) of dark blue sugarpaste into a short sausage shape and flatten both ends. Add a small handle to the side using a thin lace of paste (**D**).

5 **For the saucer** roll out 1g (⅛oz) of dark blue sugarpaste and cut out a 1.5cm (½in) circle. Push the rounded end of tool no.3 into the centre of the circle to shape it (**D**).

6 **For the plate** roll out 1g (⅛oz) of dark blue sugarpaste and cut out a 2cm (¾in) circle. Indent the top with a 1.5cm (½in) round cutter (**D**). Set all the dark blue crockery aside.

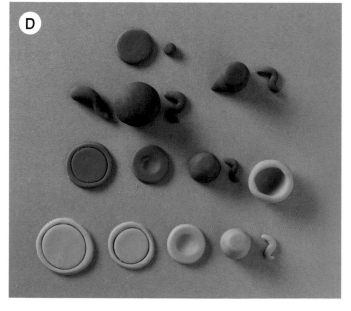

Tip
As the cup is turned upside down on the cake, it is not necessary to hollow it out.

The light blue crockery

1 For the plates roll out 20g (¾oz) of light blue sugarpaste, cut out three 3cm (1¼in) circles and indent the top of each with a 2.5cm (1in) round cutter. Cut out a further three 2.5cm (1in) circles and indent the top of each with a 2cm (¾in) round cutter. Cut out one saucer using a 1.5cm (½in) round cutter and indent the centre with tool no.3 to shape it (**D**).

2 For the bowls equally divide 10g (⅜oz) of light blue sugarpaste and roll into two balls. Push the balls over the rounded end of tool no.3 to hollow out the shapes (**D**).

3 For the cup roll 5g (¼oz) of light blue sugarpaste into a short sausage shape. Turn it upside down and flatten the top. Roll a small lace for the handle and attach to the side of the cup (**D**). Set all the light blue crockery aside.

The remaining crockery and utensils

1 Make the yellow jug and cup as for the dark blue pottery using a total of 13g (½oz) of yellow sugarpaste (**E**).

2 For the white plate roll out 5g (¼oz) of white sugarpaste and cut out a 3cm (1¼in) circle (**E**). Set aside.

3 For the washing-up liquid (dish soap) roll 7g (¼oz) of white sugarpaste into a fat sausage shape. Narrow and shape at the top and then flatten it. Using 2g (⅛oz) of green sugarpaste, take off a small ball, flatten it and attach to the top of the bottle. Add a small green cone shape on the top. Cut out a label measuring 1cm (⅜in) square and attach to the front of the bottle (**E**). Set aside.

4 For the cheese dish roll 4g (⅛oz) of cream sugarpaste into an oval shape to make the lid, pressing one end flat and sloping the other end. Using 1g (⅛oz) of red sugarpaste, take off a very small amount and roll into an oval shape for the handle. To make the dish, roll out the remainder of the red sugarpaste into a short fat sausage shape and flatten with your rolling pin (**E**). Attach the lid to the dish and set aside.

5 For the dishcloth roll out 5g (¼oz) of cream sugarpaste and cut out a 4cm (1½in) square. Using tool no.4, mark with a crisscross pattern (**E**). Crumple the shape a little and attach to the end of the sink.

6 For the dish mop roll out 2g (⅛oz) of cream sugarpaste and cut a strip measuring 1 x 5cm (⅜ x 2in). Apply a line of edible glue in the centre of the strip and place a piece of dry spaghetti on top. Fold the paste over the spaghetti, trim off the excess and roll the piece until smooth. Fill the cup of a sugar press (or garlic press) with 5g (¼oz) of white sugarpaste softened with white vegetable fat (shortening). Extrude short lengths and attach to the end of the handle (**F**). Set aside.

7 For the green spoon and spatula roll 4g (⅛oz) of green sugarpaste into a ball and then roll half the ball into a tapered cone shape. Leaving the end rounded, press it flat with your finger to form a spoon shape. Make the spatula in the same way as the spoon but cut the edge straight (**F**). Arrange all the crockery and utensils on the draining board and in the sink as desired.

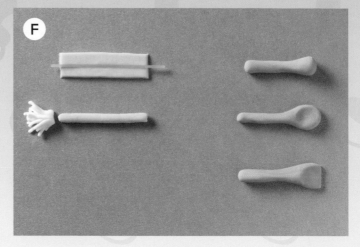

The laundry basket and laundry

1 For the basket shape 30g (1oz) of yellow sugarpaste into an oval measuring 4 x 6cm (1½ x 2⅜in). Roll out 45g (1½oz) of yellow sugarpaste to a 5mm (⅛in) thickness and cut out a rectangle measuring 3 x 23cm (1¼ x 9in). Using a straight-edged crimper, mark the piece first with vertical lines then with horizontal lines to resemble basketweave (see Crimpers) (**G**). Attach the side of the basket to the edge of the base, making a neat join at the back.

Tip
Let the basket harden off before filling it with the laundry items.

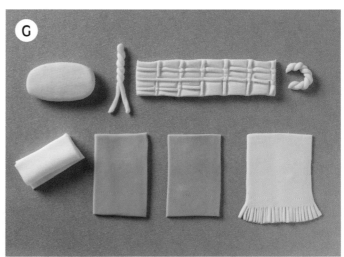

2 For the handles roll two thin laces from the leftover yellow sugarpaste and twist them together. Cut in half and attach one handle to each side of the basket (**G**).

3 For the sheets roll out 35g (1¼oz) of white sugarpaste into a rectangle measuring 14 x 5cm (5½ x 2in). Fold the sheet loosely into three and place in the basket. Using 25g (⅞oz) of light blue sugarpaste, make a second sheet measuring 10 x 5cm (4 x 2in) and place this on top of the white sheet (**G**).

4 For the blankets roll out 35g (1¼oz) of lime green sugarpaste into a rectangle measuring 14 x 5cm (5½ x 2in). Using tool no.4, fringe one end then fold it into three and place it on top of the pile. Roll out 25g (⅞oz) of jade sugarpaste into a rectangle measuring 10 x 5cm (4 x 2in) (**G**). Fold loosely and place this across the top of the lime green blanket.

Tip
Use spacers when rolling out sugarpaste to ensure an even thickness.

5 For the babygrow (romper suit) roll out 10g (⅜oz) of white sugarpaste and cut out a rectangle measuring 7 x 5cm (2¾ x 2in). Cut out the required shape with tool no.4. Soften the edges and turn up at the feet (**H**). Fold the top over and place on top of the washing.

6 For the T-shirt roll out 8g (¼oz) of red sugarpaste and cut out a rectangle measuring 5 x 3.5cm (2 x 1⅜in). Cut out the shape of the shirt and soften the edges. Roll out 1g (⅛oz) of white sugarpaste thinly and cut a narrow strip. Add to the edge of the sleeves and around the neck (**H**). Attach on top of the washing, hanging over the side of the basket.

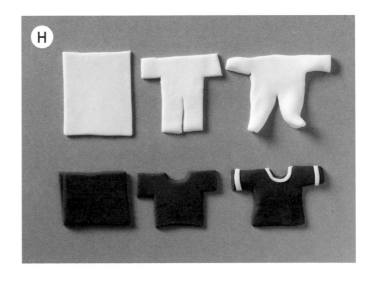

7 For the sock roll 1g (⅛oz) of pink sugarpaste into a small sausage shape and flatten with your finger, turn up one end to make the foot. Using the fine end of tool no.12, stitch mark the toe, the heel and the top of the sock (**I**). Attach to the front edge of the basket.

8 For the bib roll out 3g (⅛oz) of white sugarpaste and cut out a 3cm (1¼in) circle. Using a 1.5cm (½in) round cutter, take out a semicircle at the top. Make a thin lace with 1g (⅛oz) of light blue sugarpaste and attach around the edge of the bib, leaving extra for the ties (**I**).

9 For the hat roll 10g (⅜oz) of light blue sugarpaste into a cone shape. Fill the cup of a sugar press (or garlic press) with 5g (¼oz) of white sugarpaste softened with white vegetable fat (shortening). Extrude short strands and chop off enough to make a tassel (**I**). Attach to the top of the hat and place on the top of the washing. Secure the completed basket in front of the sink.

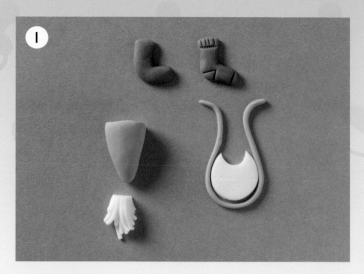

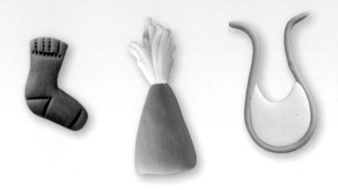

Tip
Attach the head before the arms, making it easier to secure the hands straight to the face.

The child on the potty

1 For the potty roll 25g (⅞oz) of white sugarpaste into a ball. Insert the rounded end of tool no.3 into the centre of the ball and hollow it out. Continue to shape the potty with your fingers (**J**).

2 For the body roll 25g (⅞oz) of flesh-coloured sugarpaste into a cone shape. Place on top of the potty and push a length of dry spaghetti down through the centre, leaving 2cm (¾in) showing at the top. Mark the navel with tool no.5 (**J**).

3 For the legs roll 20g (¾oz) of flesh-coloured sugarpaste into a sausage shape, turning up the foot at either end. Cut the sausage shape in half and make a diagonal cut at the top of each leg. Using tool no.4, mark the big toe and round off the edges, turning the toe upwards. Mark the four remaining toes and soften the edges. Bend the leg at the knee and shape with your fingers. Attach to the side of the body (**J**).

4 For the T-shirt roll out 4g (⅛oz) of jade sugarpaste into a strip measuring 2 x 8cm (¾ x 3⅛in). Attach around the body, making a neat seam at the back. Trim off any excess paste on the shoulders. Push a short piece of dry spaghetti into each shoulder and roll the rest of the paste into two short sausage shapes. Cut off 1.5cm (½in) from each end so that you have a rounded end and a straight end (**J**). Attach the rounded end to the top of the shoulder and push a short piece of dry spaghetti into the bottom of each sleeve.

5 For the head roll 20g (¾oz) of flesh-coloured sugarpaste into a ball and pull down the neck area by twisting the paste between your finger and thumb. Trim the neck off straight (**J**) and use the offcuts for the nose and ears. Place the head into a flower former while you work on the facial expression.

6 Add a small oval shape for the nose and mark a smile with tool no.11. Using the end of your paintbrush hollow out the mouth and pull it down to open it wide. Mark the eyes with tool no.4 by indenting a slant. Add some lines to the side of the nose and chin, and also from the eyes (**J**).

7 From 1g (⅛oz) of white sugarpaste, roll some tiny tears and attach to the face. Add a tiny oval shape for the bottom teeth and insert into the mouth. Make the ears by rolling two small teardrop shapes of leftover flesh-coloured sugarpaste and attach them to either side of the head. Indent the end of each ear with your paintbrush to secure (**J**).

8 For the hair roll 6g (¼oz) of pale yellow sugarpaste into a ball and flatten into a shape that will fit the head. Apply some edible glue around the head and attach the shape. Using tool no.4, mark the hair with lines (**J**). Slip the completed head over the spaghetti at the neck.

9 For the arms equally divide 12g (½oz) of flesh-coloured sugarpaste. Roll into two sausage shapes and narrow at each wrist. Press the rounded end on each arm flat with your finger. Model the left hand as normal (see Hands and Feet). On the right hand, mark the thumb and cut out the index finger only, softening the edges. Fold the rest of the hand into the palm, so that only the thumb and finger are now visible (**J**).

10 Bend the arms at the elbow and cut a straight edge just above (**J**). Attach over the spaghetti at the base of the sleeves. Apply some edible glue to the palms of the hands and secure over the face. Attach the child on the potty to the left-hand side of the cake board in front of the cake.

11 For the bottle roll 5g (¼oz) of white sugarpaste into a short sausage shape and flatten each end. Roll 1g (⅛oz) of light blue sugarpaste into a ball for the top and flatten with your fingertip. Attach to the top of the bottle. Roll a small cone of cream sugarpaste for the teat and secure to the top of the bottle (**J**). Place in front of the child on the potty and add a small, flattened cone of white sugarpaste for a drip of milk.

J

Tip
Refer to the section on modelling faces for more guidance on creating characters' facial expressions.

The house husband

1 For the shoes equally divide 12g (½oz) of black sugarpaste and roll into two oval shapes for the tops of the shoes. Make the soles using 5g (¼oz) of light brown sugarpaste equally divided. Roll into two sausage shapes and flatten the top ends to form the soles (**K**). Attach to the shoes and set aside.

2 For the lower body and legs roll 65g (2¼oz) of dark blue sugarpaste into a carrot shape. Place the piece on the work surface with the widest end at the bottom. Flatten the lower end, and using tool no.4, make a division for the legs two-thirds of the way up. Soften all the edges to make them smooth, lengthening the legs as you do so (**K**). Push a piece of dry spaghetti through each leg and up to the waist, leaving 2cm (¾in) showing at the top and 1cm (⅜in) showing at the bottom to attach the shoes.

Tip
Add a good pinch of CMC (Tylose) to the paste for the legs to stiffen them so they support the weight of the figure.

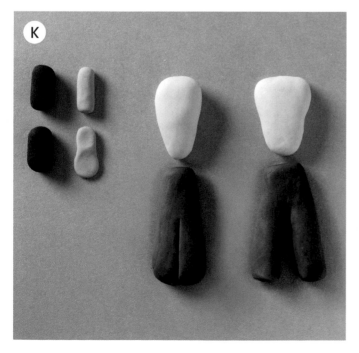

3 For the upper body roll 30g (1oz) of flesh-coloured sugarpaste into a cone shape. Turn the cone so that the thickest end is at the top. Flatten the cone and shape the shoulders, making a straight cut at the waist (**K**). Push the upper body over the spaghetti at the waistline. Stand the body in an upright position, with some support if necessary, and leave to harden off before dressing.

4 For the T-shirt roll out 40g (1½oz) of lime green sugarpaste and cut into two pieces measuring 7 x 6cm (2¾ x 2⅜in). Attach one piece to the back and bring it around to the sides. Using tool no.4, mark a straight line down the side and remove any excess paste. Cut out a 'V' at the centre top of the other piece (**L**) and attach to the front of the body, trimming off any excess to make the seam join neatly. Push a short piece of dry spaghetti into each shoulder to support the sleeves.

5 To make the collar and trim roll out 4g (⅛oz) of light blue sugarpaste and cut into a measurement of 5mm x 6cm (⅛ x 2⅜in). Make a diagonal cut in the centre, turning one half over to form the 'V' shape. Cut a further piece measuring 1 x 7cm (⅜ x 2¾in) for the collar, make a diagonal cut at the end and attach around the neck (**L**).

6 For the sleeves roll 10g (⅜oz) of lime green sugarpaste into a short sausage shape and cut in half (**L**). Attach over the spaghetti at the shoulders. Push a short piece of dry spaghetti into the bottom of each sleeve to support the arms. Stand the figure at the side of the sink and secure to the sink and the cake board with edible glue.

7 For the arms roll 16g (½oz) of flesh-coloured sugarpaste into a sausage shape. Divide in the centre, and shape the rounded ends into hands (see Hands and Feet). Bend the arms at the elbow and make a straight cut just above (**L**). Attach the right arm to the sleeve and rest it on the corner of the sink for support, leaving the fingers open to hold the mop. Set the left arm aside until you have made the baby, keeping it covered to prevent it drying out.

8 For the apron roll out 17g (½oz) of baby blue sugarpaste, cut out a rectangle measuring 7 x 6cm (2¾ x 2⅜in) and attach around the waistline. Make the ties by rolling out 1g (⅛oz) of white sugarpaste and cut into two thin strips. Lay one strip across the front of the apron and make a tie with the other, finishing with a ball for the knot (**L**).

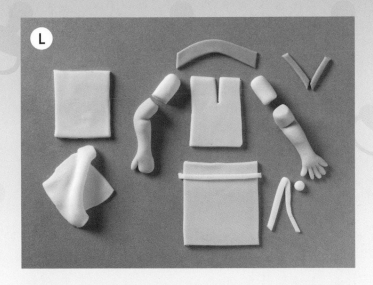

9 For the tea towel roll out 5g (¼oz) of white sugarpaste and cut out a rectangle measuring 4.5 x 5cm (1¾ x 2in). Fold the shape loosely (**L**) and drape it over the man's right shoulder.

10 For the head roll 30g (1oz) of flesh-coloured sugarpaste into a ball, pull down the neck and make a straight cut, using the offcuts for the nose and ears. For the nose, roll a small cone shape and attach to the centre of the face. Mark the nostrils with the end of a piece of dry spaghetti. Pull down the chin and mark the mouth using tool no.11. Flatten the top lip with tool no.4 and open the mouth more using the soft end of your paintbrush. Using the rounded end of tool no.4, mark the lines on either side of the nose and chin, and two in between the eyes (**M**).

11 For the eyes make two small holes just above and on either side of the nose. Roll two small balls of white sugarpaste and place inside the holes. Roll two smaller balls of dark blue sugarpaste for the irises and add on top of the white balls, looking to the right. Finally add two tiny dots of black sugarpaste for the pupils (**M**).

12 Mix a tiny amount of pink and flesh-coloured sugarpaste to get a light pink shade. Roll two small banana shapes for the lips and attach to the top and bottom of the mouth. Add two more small banana shapes of flesh-coloured sugarpaste for the eyelids and attach over the top of each eye. Add two small cone shapes for the ears and attach to the side of the head, indenting with your paintbrush to secure (**M**).

(**M**)

13 For the hair roll 16g (½oz) of light brown sugarpaste into a ball then flatten it with your fingers to fit the head. Apply some edible glue all around the head and place the hair over the back, bringing it around to the sides and top. Using the rounded end of tool no.4, mark the hair with downward strokes. To make the top piece, roll a further 2g (⅒oz) into a flattened cone shape and mark with tool no.4 as before. Attach to the top of the head, bringing it forwards and flicking up the hair at the ends (**M**).

The baby

1 For the body roll 17g (½oz) of pink sugarpaste into an oval shape. Divide the shape by marking the legs halfway down. Round off the edges to make them very smooth then turn up the foot at each end (**N**). Place the body over the left shoulder of the man and secure with edible glue. Attach the man's left arm over the spaghetti at the sleeve and secure the hand to the back of the baby.

2 For the arms roll 3g (⅛oz) of pink sugarpaste into a sausage shape and make a diagonal cut in the centre. Attach the arms to the top of the baby's body and let them hang over the man's shoulder. Equally divide 1g (⅛oz) of flesh-coloured sugarpaste, roll into two small balls for the hands and attach to the wrists. Mark the thumbs on the inside with tool no.4 (**N**).

3 For the head roll 5g (¼oz) of flesh-coloured sugarpaste into a smooth ball. Make the nose using a small amount of the flesh-coloured sugarpaste rolled into an oval shape and attach to the centre of the face. Mark a curve for the eyelids with tool no.11. Roll two small teardrop shapes for the ears and attach to the side of the head, indenting with the end of your paintbrush (**N**).

4 For the dummy (soother) roll a small ball of white sugarpaste and flatten with your finger. Attach under the nose, adding a tiny ball of pink to finish.

5 For the hair take a pinch of cream sugarpaste and roll into a thin lace. Shape into a curl and attach to the top of the head (**N**).

Tip
You can change the sex of the baby to a boy using blue sugarpaste or use any other colour you like.

The mop

1 For the handle roll out 8g (¼oz) of cream sugarpaste and cut out a strip measuring 1.5 x 14cm (½ x 5½in). Run a line of edible glue along the centre of the strip then place a length of dry spaghetti on top. Fold the paste over and trim off the excess. Roll on the work surface to reduce the thickness and trim any excess paste or spaghetti (**O**).

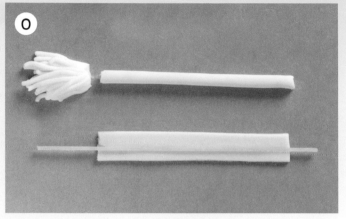

2 For the mop head soften 10g (⅜oz) of white sugarpaste with white vegetable fat (shortening) and fill the cup of a sugar press (or garlic press). Extrude lengths of paste, cut them off all together and attach to the end of the handle (**O**). Secure the mop handle to the right hand of the man with the mop head on the cake board in front of his feet and next to the laundry basket.

3 To finish the cake dust the cheeks of the three characters with plain and simple pink dust and add confectioners' glaze to highlight the shoes, eyes, teapot and the handles on the drawers and cupboards.

Tip
Experiment with the amount of white vegetable fat (shortening) needed to soften the sugarpaste in the press – it should squeeze through easily, yet hold its shape.

A Little More Fun!

Home Helpers

These matching mini cakes are made using Silverwood 5cm (2in) square mini cake pans. The effect of the sugarpaste covering is doubly effective on little cakes, which look like slabs of fine Italian marble! Top them with a square of white sugarpaste and some of the items from the main cake, such as the baby, the crockery or the washing-up items, for a lovely family-oriented treat, perfect for the end of a hard day of housework!

Father's Day

Dad stands no chance of getting a lie-in or any peace and quiet on his special day, not while the children and dog are waiting to hand over their cards and presents! This colourful and amusing design is the perfect way to celebrate Father's Day and show Dad just how much you care about him.

"Hey kids! Any chance of some breakfast in bed today?"

You will need

Sugarpaste

- ✸ 1kg 100g (2lb 6⅞oz) white
- ✸ 500g (1lb 1½oz) jade
- ✸ 255g (9oz) light green
- ✸ 111g (4oz) orange
- ✸ 86g (3oz) flesh
- ✸ 83g (3oz) grey
- ✸ 66g (2⅜oz) yellow
- ✸ 38g (1⅜oz) light blue
- ✸ 25g (⅞oz) light brown
- ✸ 20g (¾oz) dark brown
- ✸ 16g (½oz) fuchsia
- ✸ 14g (½oz) dark green
- ✸ 2g (⅛oz) dark blue
- ✸ 1g (⅛oz) red
- ✸ 1g (⅛oz) black

Materials

- ✸ 15 x 18 x 7.5cm (6 x 7 x 3in) cake
- ✸ White vegetable fat (shortening)
- ✸ Edible glue (see Recipes)
- ✸ Dry spaghetti
- ✸ Rainbow Dust: plain and simple pink

Equipment

- ✸ 25cm (10in) square cake drum
- ✸ Sugar gun
- ✸ Crimpers
- ✸ Round cutters: 2.5cm (1in), 5mm (⅛in)
- ✸ Blue ribbon 15mm (½in) wide x 1m (40in) long
- ✸ Non-toxic glue
- ✸ Basic tool kit (see General Equipment)

Covering the cake and board

1 To cover the board roll out 500g (1lb 1½oz) of jade sugarpaste to an even 3mm (⅛in) thickness. Cover the board in the usual way, trimming the edges neatly (see Covering the Cake Board). Save any leftover sugarpaste to use for the decoration. Edge the board with the blue ribbon, securing it with non-toxic glue.

2 To cover the cake roll out 800g (1lb 12¼oz) of white sugarpaste to a 5mm (⅛in) thickness and use to cover the prepared cake (see Covering Cakes and tip below). Set any leftover paste aside. Attach the cake to the centre of the cake board using edible glue mixed with sugarpaste to make a stiff paste.

Tip

When covering a square cake, secure the top edge and corners first, then smooth down the sides finishing neatly at the base.

3 **For the border around the bottom of the cake**
soften 70g (2½oz) of white sugarpaste with white
vegetable fat (shortening). Fit the three-hole disc and fill
the sugar gun, squeezing out a length of paste. Run a line
of edible glue around the bottom of the cake and attach
the border. You will have to refill the gun to make a length
long enough (**A**).

A

The pillows

1 Take 168g (6oz) of white sugarpaste and divide equally.
Knead to a smooth finish then shape with your hands into
soft rectangles. Take a crimper and pinch the edge of the
pillow around the sides and top to frill it (**A**) (see Crimpers).

2 Secure the pillows on top of the cake, placing the pillow on
the right-hand side straight and the pillow on the left-hand
side at an angle. Indent the centre of each pillow slightly.

The presents

1 **For the yellow present** shape 15g (½oz) of yellow
sugarpaste into a cube. Mix together 25g (⅞oz) of white
sugarpaste with 1g (⅛oz) of dark blue to make a light blue
shade. Roll out 6g (¼oz), cut a thin strip and attach across
the cube. Make the bow by cutting two short strips for
the tails, making a diagonal cut at each end. Attach to the
centre of the present then make two small loops, adding a
short piece across the centre to finish (**B**). Set aside.

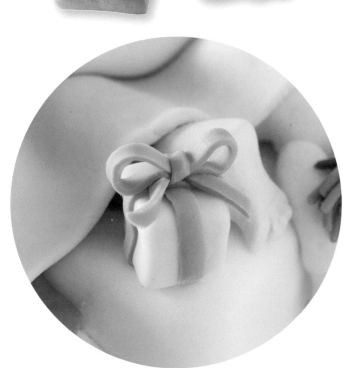

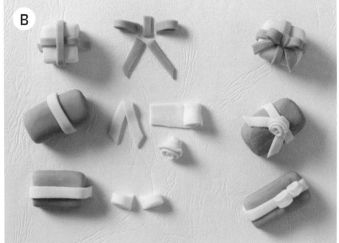

B

2 For the blue present roll the remaining pale blue sugarpaste into a rectangular prism. Roll out 5g (¼oz) of light green sugarpaste to make the ties. Cut a strip and attach it across the top half of the present. Make the tie and attach to the centre of the ribbon. Add a small rosebud to the centre by rolling out a thin strip of light green sugarpaste, roll the strip inwards into a coil and stop rolling when the rosebud is large enough. Open up the petals with your finger and attach to the centre of the ribbon (**B**). Set aside.

3 For the green present roll 14g (½oz) of dark green sugarpaste and roll into a flat rectangle shape. Using 2g (⅛oz) of white sugarpaste, make a strip to go across the present then attach two loops on the top (**B**). Set aside.

The slippers

1 For the soles mix together 3g (⅛oz) of white sugarpaste with 5g (¼oz) of light brown to make a beige shade. Take off 6g (¼oz), divide equally and roll into two smooth sausage shapes for the soles. Flatten the front of each sausage to make it wider than the back (**C**).

2 For the uppers roll out the remaining beige sugarpaste and cut into two strips measuring 1 x 2.5cm (⅜ x 1in). Attach over the front of each slipper and set aside.

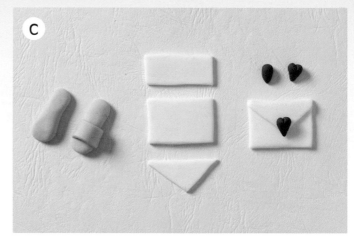

C

The Father's Day card

1 For the envelope roll out 7g (¼oz) of white sugarpaste and cut into a rectangle measuring 2 x 3cm (¾ x 1¼in) (**C**).

2 For the flap cut out another rectangle measuring 1 x 3cm (⅜ x 1¼in) and cut off the corners to make a triangle. Attach to the top of the envelope (**C**).

3 For the heart decoration roll a small cone of red sugarpaste, slightly flatten with your finger then mark the top with a line, using tool no.4, to make a heart shape. Attach the heart to the envelope and set aside (**C**).

The father

1 For the body roll 48g (1⅝oz) of orange sugarpaste into a cone shape (**D**). Place the top of the cone onto the lower edge of the left-hand pillow.

2 For the left trouser leg roll 23g (¾oz) of orange sugarpaste into a sausage shape and make a diagonal cut at the top. Make a hollow in the base of the trouser using the pointed end of tool no.3. Bend at the knee and attach to the hip, bringing the leg over the side of the cake.

3 Make the right trouser leg in the same way as the left leg using 23g (¾oz) of orange sugarpaste, attach to the right hip and place on top of the cake.

4 For the lower legs and feet equally divide 20g (¾oz) of flesh-coloured sugarpaste and roll into two short sausage shapes. Turn up one end of each sausage to make the foot and model the toes (see Hands and Feet). Push a piece of dry spaghetti into each trouser leg and apply some edible glue inside the holes. Slip the lower legs over the spaghetti, fitting them neatly inside the trousers, and secure the feet to the bed in a natural-looking position (**D**).

5 For the sleeves roll 13g (½oz) of orange sugarpaste into a sausage shape. Make a diagonal cut in the centre and hollow out the ends using tool no.3 (**D**). Push a piece of dry spaghetti into the end of each sleeve. Attach the right sleeve at the shoulder, bending it at the elbow and resting it on top of the pillow. Attach the left sleeve hanging over the side of the cake.

6 For the left lower arm roll 7g (¼oz) of flesh-coloured sugarpaste into a sausage shape, narrow at the wrist and model the hands (see Hands and Feet). Slip the arm over the spaghetti at the end of the sleeve (**D**) and attach to the side of the cake.

7 For the right hand roll 3g (⅛oz) of flesh-coloured sugarpaste into a small cone shape. Flatten the rounded end and cut out the thumb and index finger only, folding the rest of the hand inwards. Indent the folded fingers with tool no.4 (**D**). Make a straight cut at the wrist and slip over the spaghetti at the end of the sleeve, resting the hand on the pillow.

8 For the collar roll out 4g (⅛oz) of orange sugarpaste to measure 1 x 6cm (⅜ x 2⅜in). Cut out a 'V' shape at each end and then place around the neckline (**D**).

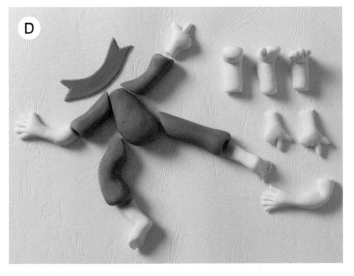

D

9 For the head roll 25g (⅞oz) of flesh-coloured sugarpaste into a ball then pull down the neck and indent the eye area (see Constructing a Head). Make a straight cut at the neck (**E**) and use the offcuts for the facial features.

10 Roll a small cone shape for the nose and attach to the centre of the face, marking the nostrils and making the opening of the mouth with tool no.5. Roll two small oval shapes for the eyelids and attach just above and on either side of the nose (**E**).

11 Using tool no.4, mark lines on each side of the nose and chin. Roll a small cone of flesh-coloured sugarpaste and insert it inside the mouth, then push tool no.5 inside the cone to open it, forming the lips. Add two small cones for the ears and secure with the end of your paintbrush (**E**).

12 For the hair soften 20g (¾oz) of dark brown sugarpaste with white vegetable fat (shortening), take off a tiny amount and roll a thin lace to outline the eyes and make the eyebrows. Fill the cup of the sugar press (or garlic press) with the remaining softened paste, extrude strands and attach to the head, keeping the style quite untidy (**E**).

E

The girl.

1 For the body roll 35g (1¼oz) of yellow sugarpaste into a cone shape (**F**) and place it at the end of the bed.

2 For the arm roll 10g (⅜oz) of yellow sugarpaste into a sausage shape, make a diagonal cut at the top and attach to the shoulder with the arm hanging over the bed (**F**).

3 For the hand roll 1g (⅛oz) of flesh-coloured sugarpaste into a cone shape and flatten slightly. Model the thumb and indent the fingers (see Hands and Feet) then push a piece of dry spaghetti into the end of the sleeve and slip the hand over (**F**).

4 For the head roll 15g (½oz) of flesh-coloured sugarpaste into a ball. Roll a tiny ball for the nose and attach to the centre of the face. Mark two holes for the eyes with tool no.5 and fill with a tiny ball of dark blue sugarpaste (**F**). Push a short piece of dry spaghetti into the top of the body and slip the head over the top so that the girl is looking down.

Tip

Because of the position of the girl's head there is no need to model the mouth, as it is not seen.

5 For the hair soften 20g (¾oz) of light brown sugarpaste with white vegetable fat (shortening) and fill the cup of the sugar press (or garlic press). Mark a line down the centre of the head to divide it. Attach the hair on either side of the line working outwards and leaving a parting (see Hairstyles). Push a short piece of dry spaghetti into each side of the head. Extrude more hair and make a bunch for each side of the head and then slip over the spaghetti (**F**).

6 For the hair ribbons roll 1g (⅛oz) of dark blue sugarpaste into a thin lace and make two tails, then make two loops and secure over the top of the lace. Add a small ball in the centre to finish. From 1g (⅛oz) of white sugarpaste roll three or four small round buttons and add to the back of the girl (**F**).

7 For the bedspread roll out 250g (8¾oz) of light green sugarpaste into a rectangle measuring 20 x 16cm (8 x 6¼in). Arrange the bedspread in disarray over the girl and the father.

The dog . . . .

1 For the body roll 35g (1¼oz) of grey sugarpaste into a cone shape (**G**) and place on top of the bedspread. Push a piece of dry spaghetti into the top of the cone to support the head.

2 For the back legs equally divide 12g (½oz) of grey sugarpaste and roll into two balls. Place the balls onto the work surface and lengthen with your finger to form the legs and feet. Attach the legs to the back of the dog and indent the paws with tool no.4 (**G**).

3 For the head roll 17g (½oz) of grey sugarpaste into a ball then narrow with your finger to shape the snout. With the end of your paintbrush, push the front of the snout upwards to make an arched shape, then pull down the cheeks with your finger (**G**).

4 For the lower jaw roll 1g (⅛oz) of grey sugarpaste into a flattened cone shape and attach under the arched shape. Roll 1g (⅛oz) of fuchsia sugarpaste into a flattened cone for the tongue and mark down the centre with tool no.4. Apply some edible glue inside the mouth and insert the tongue (**G**), then slip the head over the spaghetti onto the body, resting the head on the bedspread.

5 For the front legs roll 9g (⅜oz) of grey sugarpaste into a sausage shape. Make a diagonal cut in the centre and attach to the front of the body, indenting the paws as before. Attach the legs to the front of the body and secure the paws over the eye area. Roll a small black cone for the nose and attach to the top of the snout (**G**).

6 For the ears equally divide 4g (⅛oz) of grey sugarpaste and roll into two flattened cone shapes. Attach the ears to each side of the head (**G**).

7 For the tail roll 5g (¼oz) of grey sugarpaste into a tapered cone shape and make a diagonal cut at the thickest end. Attach to the back of the dog curling it upwards (**G**).

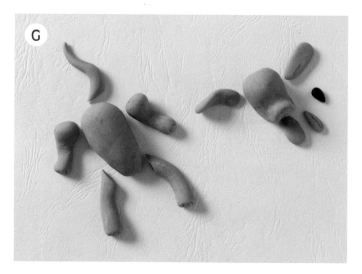

Tip
Mix some extra CMC (Tylose) powder into the paste for the dog's tail to give it more strength.

The baby

1 For the body and legs roll 32g (1oz) of light blue sugarpaste into a carrot shape and flatten it. Take tool no.4, push the point into the centre of the shape and divide it at the thickest end for the legs. Smooth the edges with your fingers then turn up the end of the legs to form the feet (**H**). Bend the figure into a sitting position and push a piece of dry spaghetti down through the body, leaving 1cm (⅜in) showing at the top.

2 For the arms roll 6g (¼oz) of light blue sugarpaste into a sausage shape and make a diagonal cut in the centre. Attach the diagonal cuts to the shoulders (**H**) and push a short piece of dry spaghetti into the wrists. Secure the figure to the top of the right-hand pillow.

3 For the hands equally divide 4g (⅛oz) of flesh-coloured sugarpaste and roll into two cone shapes. Flatten with your finger, mark the thumbs and indent the fingers (see Hands and Feet). Push the hands over the spaghetti at the wrists (**H**) and attach the left hand to the dog's tail.

4 For the bib roll out 4g (⅛oz) of white sugarpaste and cut out a 2.5cm (1in) circle. Take out a small curve at the top and secure around the neckline. Using a 5mm (⅛in) round cutter, cut out several circles to decorate the babygrow (romper suit) (**H**).

5 For the head roll 11g (⅜oz) of flesh-coloured sugarpaste into a ball. Roll a small nose and attach it to the centre of the face. Using tool no.5, make a hole for the mouth and two holes for the eyes. Roll two small balls of white sugarpaste and place inside the eye holes. Using some leftover dark blue sugarpaste, roll two tiny balls for the irises and two even tinier black balls for the pupils (**H**).

6 For the ears roll the remaining flesh-coloured sugarpaste into two small teardrop shapes and attach to each side of the head, indenting with the end of your paintbrush. Slip the head over the spaghetti at the neck (**H**).

7 For the dummy (soother) roll a tiny cone shape of white sugarpaste and insert it into the hole in the mouth then flatten it. Add a small yellow ball on the top (**H**).

8 For the hair mix 5g (¼oz) of white sugarpaste with 5g (¼oz) of yellow to make a blonde shade. Roll two banana shapes for eyebrows and attach over each eye. Soften the remaining paste with white vegetable fat (shortening) and fill the cup of a sugar press (or garlic press). Extrude short strands of hair and chop them off with tool no.4. Apply edible glue around the head and cover with hair (**H**).

The rabbit

1 **For the body** mix together 12g (½oz) of white sugarpaste with 15g (½oz) of fuchsia to make a light pink shade. Take off 11g (⅜oz) and roll into a cone shape. Mark the navel with tool no.5 (**I**).

2 **For the legs** equally divide 6g (¼oz) of the light pink sugarpaste and roll into two balls. Narrow half of each ball by rolling it on the work surface with your finger to form the leg and foot. Attach one leg to each side of the body (**I**).

3 **For the arms** roll 3g (⅛oz) of the light pink sugarpaste into a sausage shape and make a diagonal cut in the centre. Attach the arms to the top of the body (**I**) then push a short piece of dry spaghetti into the neck.

4 **For the head** roll 4g (⅛oz) of the light pink sugarpaste into a ball and slip over the spaghetti at the neck. Make a small ball for the muzzle and secure to the centre of the face. Mark a line down the centre then make a hole for the mouth with tool no.5 and mark three holes for whiskers on each side. Roll a small ball for the nose and attach at the top of the muzzle (**I**).

5 **For the ears** equally divide 2g (⅛oz) of the light pink sugarpaste and roll into two cone shapes, flattening them with your finger (**I**). Secure the rabbit to the side of the cake directly beneath the girl. Attach the ears to the side of the head, with one ear in the girl's hand.

6 Roll two small balls of white sugarpaste for the eyes and add two dots of dark blue and two smaller dots of black sugarpaste on top. Roll pads for the feet from the remaining white sugarpaste. Add two patches by rolling out 1g (⅛oz) of yellow sugarpaste and cut two small squares. Glue to the body and leg then add stitch marks all around with tool no.12 (**I**).

7 **To finish the cake** place the presents, card and slippers into position around the cake. Dust the cheeks of all the people with plain and simple pink dust.

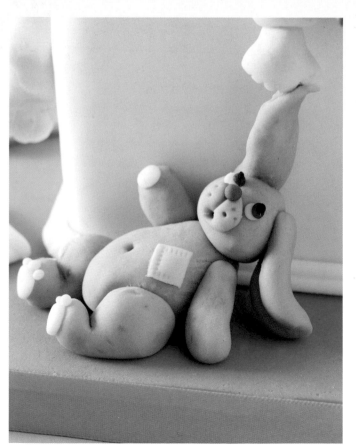

A Little More Fun!

Daddy's Delights

These matching mini cakes, baked in Silverwood 5cm (2in) square mini cake pans, make creative use of crimpers to add a simple but highly decorative effect to the edges of the sugarpaste covering (see Crimpers). Top them with motifs from the main cake such as the rabbit, present and dog, and attach an envelope on the side at an angle for a tasty treat that should help keep Dad sweet for another year!

Let It Snow

Nothing will make a man's Christmas more than a gorgeous, glamorous Miss Claus at the ready to grant all his festive wishes. This seasonal design is a nice break from tradition, with some eye-candy for the men and some playful penguins for the boys – a marvellously masculine yuletide creation!

"Sit on my knee and I'll make your Christmas wish come true!"

You will need

Sugarpaste

* 1kg 365g (3lb) white
* 800g (1lb 12¼oz) light blue
* 158g (5½oz) black
* 88g (3⅛oz) red
* 83g (3oz) flesh
* 17g (½oz) orange
* 13g (½oz) yellow
* 1g (⅛oz) dark blue
* 1g (⅛oz) pink
* 1g (⅛oz) green
* 1g (⅛oz) light brown

Materials

* 18cm (7in) square cake
* White vegetable fat (shortening)
* Icing (confectioners') sugar
* Edible glue (see Recipes)
* Dry spaghetti

Equipment

* 32cm (13in) hexagonal cake drum
* Silverwood 7.5cm (3in) round mini cake pans
* 7.5cm (3in) round silver cake card
* Round cutters: 7.5cm (3in), 7cm (2¾in), 2.5cm (1in), 1cm (⅜in), 5mm (⅛in)
* Cutting wheel (or pizza cutter)
* Textured rolling pin (optional)
* 4.5 x 3.5cm (1¾ x 1⅜in) Christmas tree cookie cutter
* Basic tool kit (see General Equipment)

Covering the board and cake

1 To cover the board roll out 625g (1lb 6oz) of white sugarpaste to an even 3mm (⅛in) thickness. Cover the board in the usual way, trimming the edges neatly (see Covering the Cake Board). Save any leftover sugarpaste for the decoration.

2 To cover the cake roll out 800g (1lb 12¼oz) of light blue sugarpaste to an even 5mm (⅛in) thickness and cover the prepared cake. Tuck in each corner first with the flat of your hand and secure the paste around the top of the cake to prevent it from stretching. Trim the lower edges neatly. Attach the cake to the centre of the cake board using edible glue mixed with sugarpaste to make a stiff paste.

The frieze

1 To complete the frieze you will need 420g (14¾oz) of white sugarpaste divided into three. Roll one portion into a smooth sausage shape 23cm (9in) long. If desired, take a small rolling pin and roll out the paste to a 5mm (⅛in) thickness, to a height of 6cm (2⅜in). Take a textured rolling pin and roll over the top of the paste. Make a straight edge at the bottom, sides and top – it should then measure 7 x 22cm (2¾ x 8⅝in).

2 Make a curved shape along the top using a cutting wheel (or pizza cutter) (**A**). Repeat with the other two portions of white sugarpaste, ensuring that they are all the same height at each end so that they will fit together. Set aside the leftover paste to make the trees.

3 Attach the first piece of the frieze to the front of the cake, turning the edges around the corner of the cake. Add the second piece, joining edge to edge with the first to make a neat join then add the third piece.

Tip
The joins in the freize will be covered by trees, so don't worry if they are not a perfect fit.

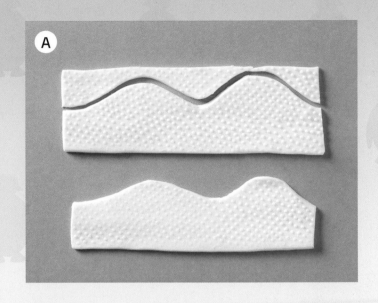

The Christmas trees

1 For the trees on the frieze roll out the leftover white sugarpaste to a 3mm (⅛in) thickness and cut out nine trees using the Christmas tree cookie cutter (**B**). Place one tree over the first join on the frieze, but elevate it 2cm (¾in) from the base of the cake, then overlap two more trees in front with the bases of these trees touching the cake board. Repeat for the other two joins on the freize.

2 For the freestanding trees on the cake board roll out 150g (5¼oz) of white sugarpaste to a 1cm (⅜in) thickness then roll over the top with the textured rolling pin, reducing the thickness to 5mm (⅛in). Cut out six trees and then push a piece of dry spaghetti through the base and up to the top of the tree, leaving 3mm (⅛in) showing at the base. Set them aside to harden off then apply some edible glue to the board and push the trees into the paste, arranging them in groups of three. Set any leftover sugarpaste aside for the snowballs (**B**).

Tip
Add a good pinch of CMC (Tylose) to the sugarpaste for the freestanding trees to firm them up.

The small penguins

1 For the body roll 16g (½oz) of black sugarpaste into a smooth cone shape. Pull out the tail at the base of the cone (**C**). Push a piece of dry spaghetti down through the cone, leaving 1cm (⅜in) showing at the top.

2 For the chest roll 1g (⅛oz) of white sugarpaste into a small cone shape and flatten with your rolling pin (**C**). Attach to the front of the penguin.

3 For the feet equally divide 3g (⅛oz) of orange sugarpaste, roll into two small cones and flatten. Using tool no.4, mark two lines on each cone for the claws (**C**) and attach to the body.

4 For the wings equally divide 4g (⅛oz) of black sugarpaste and roll into two cone shapes. Flatten slightly with your finger and attach the widest end of each cone to the top of the body, shaping into the required position (**C**).

C

5 For the head roll 8g (¼oz) of black sugarpaste into a small ball. Attach to the top of the body. Roll a small cone of yellow sugarpaste for the beak and flatten at the end. Attach to the centre of the face. Add two small balls of white sugarpaste for the eyes, adding two tiny dots of black sugarpaste on the top. From 1g (⅛oz) of black sugarpaste, roll three thin tapered cone shapes for the hair and attach to the top of the head (**C**).

6 Make three penguins, arranging them in different positions on the board. Roll a few snowballs with the leftover white sugarpaste and place around the board.

Miss Claus's seat

1 cover the mini cake by rolling 130g (4½oz) of white sugarpaste into a sausage shape 28cm (11in) long and 5mm (⅛in) thick. If desired, roll over the top with a textured rolling pin. Make a straight edge at the base and top of the strip – it should now measure 6.5 x 28cm (2½ x 11in). Attach around the prepared cake, making a neat join at the back. Re-roll the paste and texture it, then cut out a 7.5cm (3in) circle and place on the top (**D**).

2 Secure the cake onto the silver cake card and trim if there is any card showing.

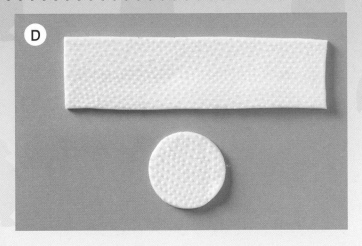

Tip
If you want to save Miss Claus as a keepsake, make the seat from a 7.5cm (3in) round cake dummy instead.

Miss Claus

1 For the lower body roll 35g (1¼oz) of red sugarpaste into a cone shape. Make a straight cut at the top then, using the large rounded end of tool no.3, push out what will be half of the bust area at the top of the body shape (**E**). Place the lower body on top of the seat and insert a piece of dry spaghetti down through the centre and into the cake, leaving 2cm (¾in) showing at the top.

2 For the boots equally divide 14g (½oz) of red sugarpaste and roll into two sausage shapes. Turn up the end of each boot, mark the heel across the back with tool no.4 and pull the heel down with your fingers (**E**). Push a length of dry spaghetti down into the boot, leaving 2cm (¾in) showing at the top and set aside.

3 For the legs equally divide 28g (1oz) of flesh-coloured sugarpaste and roll into two smooth sausage shapes, narrowing at the back of each knee and ankle area to form the calf shape. Bend each leg at the knee, make a diagonal cut at the top and a straight cut below the knee (**E**). Slip the boots onto the end of each leg. Position the right leg on the seat with the left leg crossed over, resting on the cake.

Tip
Place the legs in a natural-looking position — some CMC (Tylose) will help firm them up.

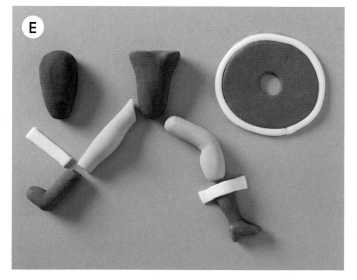

4 Trim each boot by rolling out 2g (⅛oz) of white sugarpaste into a strip measuring 1 x 4cm (⅜ x 1½in) and attach across the join at the top of each boot (**E**).

5 For the skirt roll out 30g (1oz) of red sugarpaste and cut out a 7cm (2¾in) circle. Take out a further 2.5cm (1in) circle in the centre (**E**). Slip the skirt over the top of the body and secure around the waistline. Lift the frills around the edges with the end of your paintbrush to give it movement.

6 For the skirt trim roll out 3g (⅛oz) of white sugarpaste into a lace. Flatten slightly with your finger then apply a line of edible glue around the edge of the skirt and attach, making a neat join at the back (**E**).

7 For the upper body roll 15g (½oz) of flesh-coloured sugarpaste into a ball then pull up the neck with your fingers. Pull out the arms to the elbows at the sides by gently rolling them with your fingers. Make a ridge across the bustline by pushing up the paste in between your fingers. Mark the ridge in the centre then round off the bust until you have a nice shape. Attach the upper body to the lower body, shaping the bust into a natural-looking shape at the top. Bend the arms downwards and make a straight cut at the elbow (**F**). Push a short piece of dry spaghetti into the end of each arm to take the gloves.

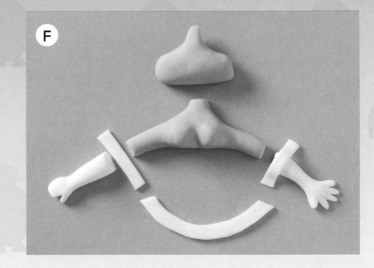

8 For the gloves equally divide 12g (½oz) of white sugarpaste and roll into two sausage shapes. Narrow each shape at the wrist, flatten the end slightly and model the fingers (see Hands and Feet). Attach the gloves over the spaghetti at the end of the arms, and rest on the skirt.

9 For the cuffs roll out 2g (⅛oz) of white sugarpaste and cut a strip measuring 6mm x 6cm (¼ x 2⅜in), cut in half and attach over the join between the arms and the gloves (**F**).

10 For the neckline trim roll out 4g (⅛oz) of white sugarpaste and cut a strip measuring 6mm x 15cm (¼ x 6in) (**F**). Attach all the way around the neckline and finish at the back with a neat join.

11 For the head roll 30g (1oz) of flesh-coloured sugarpaste into a smooth ball then pull down the neck from the base, rolling it in between your fingers. Place the head into the palm of your hand, and with your little finger indent the eye area (see Constructing a Head). Make a straight cut at the neck (**G**) and save the offcuts for the nose and ears.

12 For the nose and mouth attach a small cone shape for the nose and indent the nostrils with tool no.5. Mark a line down each side of the nose with tool no.4. Mark the mouth with tool no.11. Flatten the top of the smile then open the mouth a little with the soft end of your paintbrush (**G**).

13 For the teeth and lips roll a small tapered sausage shape of white sugarpaste for the teeth and insert under the top of the mouth along the straight line. Roll two small tapered sausage shapes of pink sugarpaste for the lips and attach at the top and bottom of the mouth. (**G**).

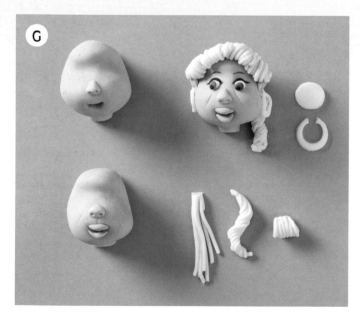

14 For the ears and earrings roll two small teardrop shapes for the ears from the leftover flesh-coloured sugarpaste and attach on either side of the head, indenting the base of each ear with the end of your paintbrush. Roll out 1g (⅛oz) of white sugarpaste and cut out two 1cm (⅜in) circles. Take out the centre using a 5mm (⅛in) round cutter to form a ring, then split the ring and attach to the ears (**G**).

15 For the eyes roll two tiny balls of white sugarpaste and attach one on either side of the nose. Add two even smaller balls of dark blue sugarpaste on the top, and two tiny dots of black for the pupils. Decide which direction you want her to be looking in. Roll two thin arched laces of light brown sugarpaste and attach over the eyes for the eyebrows and two thin laces of black to outline the top of the eyes.

Let it Snow

16 For the hair mix 10g (⅜oz) of flesh-coloured sugarpaste with 10g (⅜oz) of yellow to make a light blonde shade. Soften this paste with white vegetable fat (shortening) and fill the cup of the sugar press (or garlic press). Extrude long strands and twist four or five strands together to make the long curls. Attach behind the ear and bring forwards over the shoulder. Refill the press and extrude shorter strands, taking off several at a time and folding them over around the front. To complete the hair, add short strands from the neck to the crown and around the sides (**G**).

17 For the hat roll 3g (⅛oz) of red sugarpaste into a tapered cone shape. Flatten out the widest end with your fingers so that it fits the head. Roll 3g (⅛oz) of white sugarpaste into a strip measuring 1 x 10cm (⅜ x 4in) and attach around the edge of the hat. Bring the top over to the side and attach it to the head adding a small ball of white to the end (**H**).

18 For the holly leaf and berry decoration divide 1g (⅛oz) of green sugarpaste into three and roll into cone shapes. Flatten and mark with tool no.4 to look like holly leaves. Attach to the hat trim at the side of the head. Roll three small balls of red sugarpaste for berries and place in the centre (**H**).

19 Dowel the base cake (see Dowelling Cakes) then lift the completed Miss Claus on her seat onto the top of the large cake and secure with edible glue.

Tip
Avoid piling the hair too high at the top otherwise it will elevate the hat too much.

The larger penguins

1 Make two penguins as described for the three small penguins on the board, but using the following amounts of sugarpaste: 20g (¾oz) of black for the body, 5g (¼oz) of black equally divided for the wings, 2g (⅛oz) of white for the chest, 10g (⅜oz) of black for the head, 1g (⅛oz) of yellow for the beak, 4g (⅛oz) of orange equally divided for the feet.

2 For the hat take 2g (⅛oz) of red sugarpaste and make into a long cone shape. Flatten the wide end with your fingers to fit the head. Roll 1g (⅛oz) of white sugarpaste into a strip and attach around the edges. Push a short piece of dry spaghetti into the tip of the hat and add a small white ball to the end (**H**). Attach to the head of one penguin.

3 For the bow roll out 1g (⅛oz) of red sugarpaste and cut into a very thin strip. Divide into four pieces, using two for the ties. Loop the other two pieces to form the bow, adding a small ball in the centre to finish (**I**). Attach to the neck of the penguin with the hat.

4 For the candy cane roll 1g (⅛oz) of white sugarpaste and 1g (⅛oz) of red into thin laces. Twist together then shape the cane, trim both ends and set aside to harden off.

5 Position the penguin with the hat at the front of the cake looking up at Miss Claus and place the other penguin at the back holding the candy cane. Complete the scene with three snowballs rolled from 1g (⅛oz) of white sugarpaste and lightly dust around the cake with icing (confectioners') sugar.

Tip

If your twists start to crack, add some white vegetable fat (shortening) to the sugarpaste.

Let it Snow

A Little More Fun!

Antarctic Antics

These penguin cakes, baked in Silverwood 7.5cm (3in) round mini cake pans, will bring a real sense of joy to any festive celebration, and would be great to make on their own if time is short. Model the penguins as on the main cake, and have fun positioning them doing amusing things. Use a border of snowballs and a Christmas tree to complete the wintery scene.

Whole Nine Yards

If you are willing to go the distance for the man in your life, then he will love you for making this humorous take on his favourite all-action sport. This cake is totally customizable and can be adapted for any age of sports fan just by changing the numbers. You could also try using letters to spell out his name or a birthday message.

"This cake is in the major league – it's really in the zone!"

You will need

Sugarpaste

- ★ 1kg (2lb 3¼oz) light green
- ★ 600g (1lb 5oz) dark green
- ★ 521g (1lb 2⅜oz) white
- ★ 194g (6¾oz) red
- ★ 194g (6¾oz) grey
- ★ 176g (6¼oz) dark brown
- ★ 114g (4oz) blue
- ★ 54g (2oz) flesh
- ★ 14g (½oz) black

Materials

- ★ 20cm (8in) square cake
- ★ White vegetable fat (shortening)
- ★ Dry spaghetti
- ★ Edible glue (see Recipes)

Equipment

- ★ 20cm (12in) square cake drum
- ★ 1cm (⅜in) star cutter
- ★ Numbers cutters or templates (see Templates)
- ★ Red ribbon 15mm (½in) wide x 120cm (47in) long
- ★ Non-toxic glue
- ★ Basic tool kit (see General Equipment)

Covering the cake and board

1 To cover the board roll out 600g (1lb 5oz) of dark green sugarpaste to an even 3mm (⅛in) thickness. Cover the board in the usual way (see Covering the Cake Board), trimming the edges neatly. Edge the board with the red ribbon, securing it with non-toxic glue.

2 To cover the cake roll out 1kg (2lb 3¼oz) of light green sugarpaste to an even 5mm (⅛in) thickness and cover the prepared cake. Tuck in each corner first with the flat of your hand and secure the paste around the top of the cake to prevent it from stretching. Trim the lower edges neatly. Attach the cake to the centre of the cake board using edible glue mixed with sugarpaste to make a stiff paste.

Tip
Roll some leftover sugarpaste into a ball and use to polish the top of the cake. This will provide a nice smooth surface and help remove any imperfections.

The side decoration

1 To make the stripes roll out 60g (2oz) of white sugarpaste and 60g (2oz) of red and cut each colour into four strips measuring 13mm x 25cm (½ x 10in) (**A**). Apply a line of edible glue around the base of the cake and attach to each side of the cake, making a neat join at each corner.

2 For the birthday numbers roll out 100g (3½oz) of blue sugarpaste to an even 6mm (¼in) thickness. Cut out the required numbers using cutters or the templates supplied (see Templates), then place the numbers down on to a flat surface.

3 For the stars thinly roll out 10g (⅜oz) of white sugarpaste. Using a 1cm (⅜in) star cutter, press out ten stars and secure to the top of the numbers (**A**) then attach to the centre front of the cake.

Tip
Different numbers will need more or fewer stars so experiment to see what looks best.

4 For the footballs equally divide 120g (4¼oz) of dark brown sugarpaste into four and roll into balls. Shape the balls into tapered sausage shapes and stitch mark a line down the centre of each ball with tool no.12. Thinly roll out 4g (⅛oz) of white sugarpaste and cut a narrow strip to be placed on top of each ball. Cut a fine strip for the laces and cut into six short pieces (**A**). Attach across the top of each ball, securing with edible glue.

5 Make a smaller football for the top of the cake in the same way using 20g (¾oz) of dark brown sugarpaste and 1g (⅛oz) of white sugarpaste and set aside until required.

The red-team player number one.

Note: This player is at the bottom of the scrum – his legs, arms and helmet are all that are visible on the finished cake.

1 For the lower body and thighs roll 80g (2⅞oz) of white sugarpaste into a cone shape and flatten slightly with your hand. Divide the widest end to form the legs and smooth the edges, making them very rounded with your fingers. Push the paste together to form a ridge across the lower body then shape it for the cheeks of his rear, rounding them off with your finger. Push a piece of dry spaghetti into the end of each thigh to support the lower legs. Make a straight cut at the waist (**B**).

Tip
Keep the thighs nice and chunky when you are rolling them.

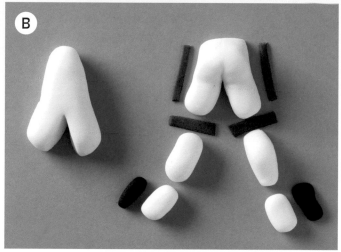

2 For the lower legs equally divide 30g (1oz) of white sugarpaste into two sausage shapes. Narrow each end by rolling it on the work surface – this should form the bulging calf muscle in the centre – then make a straight cut at each end (**B**). Slip the lower legs over the spaghetti at the thighs. Push a short piece of dry spaghetti into the bottom end to support the boots.

3 For the boots equally divide 12g (½oz) of white sugarpaste and roll into two oval shapes to form the uppers. Take 3g (⅛oz) of black sugarpaste and divide equally for the soles. Roll into two small sausage shapes and flatten with your finger, making the top half of each wider. Attach the soles to the boots and mark a line across for the heels with tool no.4 (**B**). Slip the boots over the spaghetti at the end of the legs.

4 For the trim roll out 4g (⅛oz) of red sugarpaste and cut a thin strip to go down each side of the trousers from the waist to the knee. Cut a wider strip to go around the join at each knee to form the top of the sock (**B**).

5 For the upper body roll 35g (1¼oz) of red sugarpaste into a fat cone shape (**C**), make a straight cut at the widest end and attach to the lower body. Keeping the figure flat on the work surface, push a short piece of dry spaghetti into each shoulder then position the figure face down on top of the cake.

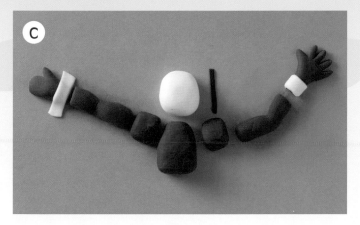

6 For the arms equally divide 36g (1¼oz) of dark brown sugarpaste and roll into two sausage shapes. Narrow each shape at the wrist and inside the bend of the arm, making the muscles stand out (**C**). Bend the left arm at the elbow and make a straight cut at the wrist, then push a short piece of dry spaghetti into the end to support the glove. Attach the left arm over the spaghetti at the shoulder, with the elbow resting on the top of the cake and the forearm very upright to hold the ball. Set the right arm aside.

7 For the gloves equally divide 8g (¼oz) of red sugarpaste and roll into two cone shapes. Flatten the end and model the fingers (see Hands and Feet) (**C**). Set the right glove aside. Slip the left glove over the spaghetti at the wrist on the left arm, keeping the palm open. Push a piece of spaghetti down through the palm of this hand, through the arm and into the cake, leaving 2cm (¾in) showing in the palm to support the ball.

Tip

When making the gloves, place them together and mark the thumbs on the inside – this will ensure that you get a right and a left hand.

8 For the wristbands roll out 2g (⅛oz) of white sugarpaste and cut into two strips (**C**). Attach one strip around the join between the left glove and arm and set the other strip aside.

9 Slip the football made earlier over the spaghetti in the left hand and secure the fingers around it with edible glue. Secure the right arm into place, keeping it bent at the elbow. Attach the right glove and the wristband.

10 For the shoulder pads equally divide 20g (¾oz) of red sugarpaste, shape into two ovals and place one over the top of each arm (**C**).

11 For the helmet roll 34g (1⅛oz) of white sugarpaste into a ball. Push a piece of dry spaghetti into the top of the body and attach the helmet. Roll out 1g (⅛oz) of black sugarpaste, cut a very thin stripe and attach to the top (**C**).

The red-team player number two

1 Make all the parts exactly as described for red-team player number one using 80g (2⅞oz) of white for the lower body and thighs, 30g (1oz) of white for the lower legs, 12g (½oz) of white for the boots with 3g (⅛oz) of black for the soles, 4g (⅛oz) of red for the trim, 35g (1¼oz) of red for the upper body, 36g (1¼oz) of flesh for the arms, 8g (¼oz) of red for the gloves, 2g (⅛oz) of white for the wristbands, 20g (¾oz) of red for the shoulder pads, 34g (1⅛oz) of white for the helmet and 1g (⅛oz) of black for the helmet stripe.

2 Place the lower body and legs over red-team player number one, arranging the legs into the position shown (see tip below). Attach the left hand to the football and the right arm resting on the helmet of the red-team player number one.

Tip

Support the legs in the required position with foam until dry.

The blue-team player number one

1 Make the lower body, legs and boots as for red-team player number two, using the quantities given above, except using 80g (2⅞oz) of grey sugarpaste for the lower body and thighs and 4g (⅛oz) of blue sugarpaste for the trim (**D**). Position the body across the right arm of red-team player number one, keeping the legs apart.

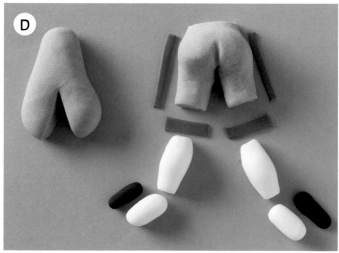

2 Make the upper body as for red-team player number two, but using 35g (1¼oz) of white sugarpaste for the body, 18g (¾oz) of flesh-coloured sugarpaste to make the left arm only, 10g (⅜oz) of white for the left shoulder pad only, 4g (⅛oz) of blue for the glove and 1g (⅛oz) of white for the wristband (**E**). Position the hand in front of the player so that the helmet will rest on it.

3 Make the helmet as for red-team player number two but using 34g (1⅛oz) of grey sugarpaste. Roll out 2g (⅛oz) of blue sugarpaste, cut a very thin strip into a 'V' shape and attach over the top of the helmet (**E**).

The blue-team player number two

Note: This player is seen only from the waist downwards, so you do not need to make the upper body.

Make the lower body, legs and boots as for blue-team player number one. Slope the paste on the upper body so that it will slip underneath red-team player number one, trimming off any excess if necessary. Push a longer length of dry spaghetti into the end of the right leg and up into the thigh to keep it in an upright position. Support with foam if necessary until dry.

Hobby-Mad Minis

Among this collection of mini cakes there is surely a design that will suit the man of the moment. Whether he plays golf, football or cricket, is an avid spectator of racing or tennis, or simply loves to drop a line and wait for a bite, be inspired to get creative, either on a small cake or by scaling up the designs for a larger cake.

"I'm the one that didn't get away! These cakes make a real splash!"

You will need

Sugarpaste

★ 135g (4¾oz) blue
★ 28g (1oz) red
★ 4g (⅛oz) white
★ 3g (⅛oz) grey
★ 2g (⅛oz) black
★ 1g (⅛oz) brown

Materials

★ 6.5cm (2½in) round mini cake
★ Edible glue (see Recipes)

Equipment

★ Silverwood 6.5cm (2½in) round mini cake pans
★ 6.5cm (2½in) round silver cake card
★ 3cm (1¼in) round cutter
★ Pimpled impression mats
★ Basic tool kit (see General Equipment)

Tee Time . . . .

1 To cover the cake roll out the blue sugarpaste to an even 5mm (⅛in) thickness and cover the prepared cake, trimming the edges neatly. Attach the cake to the cake card and trim if there is any card showing.

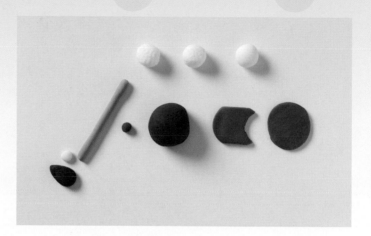

2 For the golf cap roll 20g (¾oz) of red sugarpaste into a ball. Push the end of a small rolling pin into the paste and smooth around the top of the pin. Place on top of the cake.

3 For the peak roll out the remaining red sugarpaste, not too thinly, and cut out a 3cm (1¼in) circle. Using the same cutter, take out one-third of the circle to shape the peak. Attach to the front of the hat.

4 For the trim roll out 2g (⅛oz) of black sugarpaste and cut out a thin strip to trim the peak. Then cut two small triangles and attach one to either side of the hat with edible glue. Finally, roll a small oval, flatten it with your finger and attach to the front of the hat.

5 For the golf balls take 3g (⅛oz) of white sugarpaste and divide equally into three. Roll each into a smooth ball then place in between two impression mats and make a circular movement – this will leave a pattern on the surface of each ball. Attach to the top of the cake.

6 For the golf club roll 3g (⅛oz) of grey sugarpaste into a very thin lace for the handle and attach to the front of the cake. Make the wood by rolling 1g (⅛oz) of brown sugarpaste into a flattened cone shape and attach to the end. Roll one further small ball of white sugarpaste and attach just above the head of the golf club.

You will need

Sugarpaste

★ 155g (5½oz) white
★ 60g (2oz) green
★ 35g (1¼oz) black

Materials

★ 7cm (2¾in) mini ball cake
★ Edible glue (see Recipes)
★ Buttercream (see Recipes)
★ White vegetable fat (shortening)
★ Confectioners' glaze

Equipment

★ 7cm (2¾in) Silverwood mini hemisphere cake pans
★ 7.5cm (3in) round silver cake card
★ 1.5cm (½in) hexagon cutter
★ Basic tool kit (see General Equipment)

Soccer Star

1 **To cover the cake** sandwich the two halves of the ball cake together and cover with buttercream. Place the cake onto a piece of greaseproof (wax) paper. Roll out 120g (4¼oz) of white sugarpaste to an even 5mm (⅛in) thickness and place over the top of the ball, shaping it down to the base and trimming the edges neatly.

2 **For the hexagon pattern** roll out 35g (1¼oz) of white and 35g (1¼oz) of black sugarpaste to an even 3mm (⅛in) thickness. Cut out the shapes using the hexagon cutter and attach them in sequence as shown.

3 **For the grass** cover the cake card with 30g (1oz) of green sugarpaste rolled out to an even thickness and trim the edges neatly. Mix some leftover green sugarpaste with edible glue to make a stiff paste and use to attach the cake centrally on the cake card. Soften a further 30g (1oz) of green sugarpaste with white vegetable fat (shortening) and fill the cup of a sugar press (or garlic press). Apply some edible glue to the covered cake card. Extrude short strands of grass and use tool no.4 to chop off clumps and arrange around the football.

You will need

Sugarpaste

* 140g (5oz) green
* 7g (¼oz) light brown
* 3g (⅛oz) white
* 2g (⅛oz) black
* 2g (⅛oz) red

Materials

* 5cm (2in) square mini cake
* Edible glue (see Recipes)
* Dry spaghetti
* Confectioners' glaze

Equipment

* 5cm (2in) Silverwood square mini cake pans
* 7.5cm (3in) square silver cake card
* Basic tool kit (see General Equipment)

Cricket Crazy

1 To cover the cake roll out the green sugarpaste to an even 5mm (⅛in) thickness and cover the prepared cake, trimming the edges neatly. Attach the cake to the cake card and trim if there is any card showing.

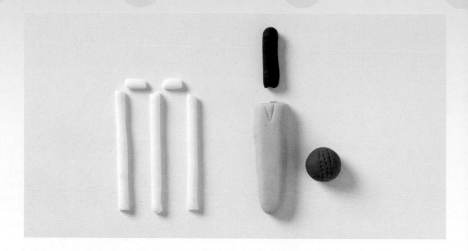

2 For the stumps roll the white sugarpaste into a lace measuring 20cm (8in) long. Take a length of dry spaghetti and push through the centre, from one end to the other. Trim off three 6cm (2⅜in) lengths.

3 For the bales roll the remaining white sugarpaste into a small sausage shape. Cut in half and mark with three lines using tool no.4. Attach the stumps to the front of the cake, spacing them with the bales.

4 For the cricket bat roll the light brown sugarpaste into a sausage shape measuring 5 x 1.5cm (2 x ½in). Flatten out the front of the bat and make a ridge at the back, making a straight cut at the top. Using tool no.4, lightly press a 'V' shape at the top of the bat. Push a length of dry spaghetti down through the centre leaving 3cm (1¼in) showing at the top.

5 For the handle roll the black sugarpaste into a small sausage shape and slip over the spaghetti at the top of the bat. Using tool no.4, mark horizontal lines across the handle.

6 For the ball roll the red sugarpaste into a smooth ball. Using tool no.12, press three lines of stitch marks around the centre. Secure the bat and ball to the top of the cake with edible glue.

7 To finish coat the handle on the cricket bat and the ball with confectioners' glaze.

You will need

Sugarpaste

* ✴ 143g (5oz) white
* ✴ 38g (1⅜oz) red
* ✴ 20g (¾oz) blue

Materials

* ✴ 7cm (2¾in) mini ball cake
* ✴ Edible glue (see Recipes)
* ✴ Buttercream (see Recipes)
* ✴ Black food colour pen

Equipment

* ✴ 7cm (2¾in) Silverwood mini hemisphere cake pans
* ✴ 7.5cm (3in) round silver cake card
* ✴ 1cm (⅜in) star cutter
* ✴ Flag shape template (see Templates)
* ✴ Basic tool kit (see General Equipment)

Baseball Classic · · · · · · · · · · · · · · · · · ·

1 Cover the cake card with 30g (1oz) of red sugarpaste, trimming the edges neatly. Make a twist to go around the edge of the card by rolling 15g (½oz) of blue and 15g (½oz) of white sugarpaste into laces. Twist together, apply a line of edible glue around the edge of the card and attach the twist then set aside.

2 To cover the cake sandwich the two halves of the ball cake together and cover with buttercream. Place the cake onto a piece of greaseproof (wax) paper. Roll out 120g (4¼oz) of white sugarpaste to an even 5mm (⅛in) thickness and place over the top of the ball, shaping it down to the base and trimming the edges neatly.

3 For the flag place the flag shape template (see Templates) on top of the ball and use a straight pin to mark out the shape with a series of dots. Roll out 5g (¼oz) of blue sugarpaste and cut out to a measurement of 2.5 x 4.5cm (1 x 1¾in) then round off the top left-hand corner. Attach to the top of the cake within the marked-out shape.

4 For the stars and stripes cut out the stars from the leftover white sugarpaste and attach to the blue part of the flag. Thinly roll out 8g (¼oz) of white and 8g (¼oz) of red sugarpaste and cut into lengths 7mm (¼in) wide. Adjust the length of each strip so that it disappears under the cake.

5 For the stitching once the design is firmly in place, draw on the stitching with a black food colour pen. Using tool no.5, mark holes on the outside edges of each stitch.

6 To finish mix some leftover red sugarpaste with edible glue to make a stiff paste and use to attach the cake centrally on the cake card.

Sugarpaste

* 145g (5⅛oz) green
* 15g (½oz) white
* 10g (⅜oz) blue
* 6g (¼oz) grey
* 6g (¼oz) yellow
* 2g (⅛oz) black

Materials

* 5cm (2in) square mini cake
* Edible glue (see Recipes)
* White vegetable fat
  (shortening)
* Dry spaghetti
* Confectioners' glaze

Equipment

* 5cm (2in) Silverwood
  square mini cake pans
* 7.5cm (3in) square
  silver cake card
* 2.5cm (1in) round cutter
* Basic tool kit (see
  General Equipment)

Love–Forty

1 To cover the cake roll out the green sugarpaste to an even 5mm (⅛in) thickness and cover the prepared cake, tucking in the corners first to prevent any stress in the paste. Trim the base neatly and round off the corners. Set any leftover green sugarpaste aside to make the grass. Attach centrally on a 7.5cm (3in) square cake card.

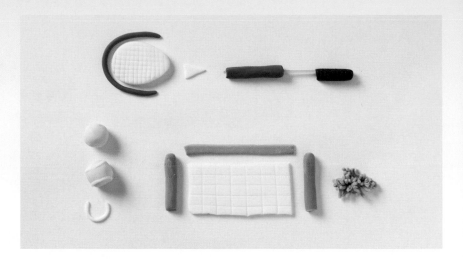

2 For the net roll out 5g (¼oz) of white sugarpaste and cut to a measurement of 2.5 x 5cm (1 x 2in). Attach to the front of the cake and mark with horizontal and vertical lines using tool no.4. Roll out 1g (⅛oz) of grey sugarpaste and cut a thin strip 5cm (2in) long for the top of the net. Roll 5g (¼oz) of grey sugarpaste into a sausage shape 7cm (2¾in) long. Cut in half and attach to each side of the net.

3 For the grass soften the leftover green sugarpaste with white vegetable fat (shortening) and fill the cup of a sugar press (or garlic press). Extrude short strands of grass, chop of into clumps with tool no.4 and attach around the edge of the cake with edible glue, covering the visible cake card.

4 For the tennis racquet roll out 8g (¼oz) of white sugarpaste to a 5mm (⅛in) thickness. Cut out a 2.5cm (1in) circle for the centre of the racquet. Shape the circle into a petal shape by pulling out the lower edge slightly. Using tool no.4, mark the strings with horizontal and vertical lines. Roll 2g (⅛oz) of blue sugarpaste into a very fine lace and attach around the edge of the racquet.

5 For the handle roll a further 2g (⅛oz) of blue sugarpaste into a short sausage shape. Push a piece of dry spaghetti through the handle and into the centre of the racquet for support. Cut out a small white triangle and attach to the top of the handle.

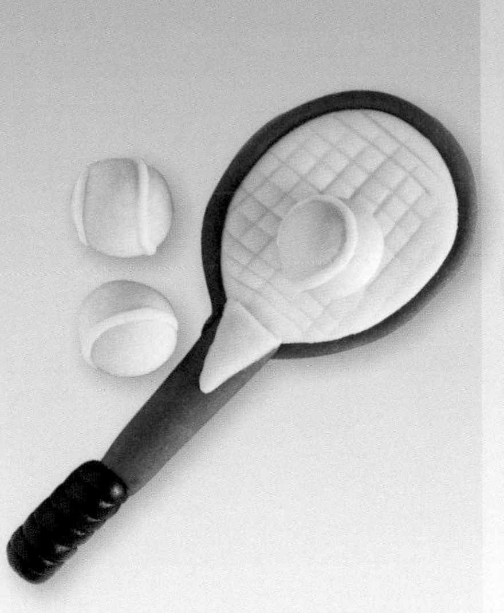

6 **For the grip** roll 2g (⅛oz) of black sugarpaste into a short sausage shape. Make a straight cut at one end and attach to the handle. Mark lines across using tool no.4. Keep the completed racquet flat until dry.

7 **For the tennis balls** make a lime green shade by mixing 6g (¼oz) of blue sugarpaste with 6g (¼oz) of yellow. Take off 2g (⅛oz) and roll into a ball. Flatten the ball and attach above the net on the side of the cake. Divide the remaining lime green sugarpaste into three and roll into smooth balls. Roll out 1g (⅛oz) of white sugarpaste into a very fine lace and cut fine strips to go around the balls.

8 **To finish** place the tennis racquet on top of the cake and add the balls, securing with edible glue. Paint the handle on the racquet with confectioners' glaze.

You will need

Sugarpaste

- 116g (4oz) white
- 60g (2oz) pale blue
- 21g (¾oz) orange
- 20g (¾oz) dark blue
- 7g (¼oz) yellow
- 1g (⅛oz) black

Materials

- 6.5cm (2½in) round mini cake
- Edible glue (see Recipes)
- Dry spaghetti
- Rainbow Dust: white hologram

Equipment

- 6.5cm (2½in) Silverwood round mini cake pans
- 6.5cm (2½in) round silver cake card
- Round cutters: 3cm (1¼in), 2.5cm (1in)
- Decorative ribbon 15mm (½in) wide x 26cm (10¼in) long
- Basic tool kit (see General Equipment)

Gone Fishin'

1 **To cover the cake** randomly mix together 65g (2¼oz) of white, 60g (2oz) of pale blue and 20g (¾oz) of dark blue sugarpaste. Roll out to an even 5mm (⅛in) thickness and cover the prepared cake, trimming the edges neatly. Attach the cake to the cake card and trim if there is any card showing.

2 **For the splash** roll out 20g (¾oz) of white sugarpaste to a 6mm (¼in) thickness, cut out a circle for the base using a 3cm (1¼in) round cutter and attach to the top of the cake. Use a further 30g (¾oz) of white sugarpaste to make the splashes. Take off 3g (⅛oz) and roll into a cone shape, push a short piece of dry spaghetti into the narrow end, through the centre, but not quite up to the top, leaving some spaghetti showing at the bottom of the shape. Push the spaghetti into the base and secure with edible glue. Continue to make more of these cone shapes, making some larger than others, and attach around the edge of the base.

3 Complete the splash using the remaining white sugarpaste. Roll a sausage shape to fit around the base and push the end of your paintbrush into it, to make rough water. Add a few small dots on the top of the splashes. Dust the splash with white hologram dust to make it sparkle.

4 For the fish's body roll 20g (¾oz) of orange sugarpaste into a cone shape, turning up the narrow end.

5 For the tail fins roll 2g (⅛oz) of yellow sugarpaste into a flattened cone shape. Using tool no.4, make a small cut in the centre top and soften the edges. Mark curved lines on the tail with the edge of a round cutter. Push a short piece of dry spaghetti into the end of the fish's body and slip the tail over the top.

6 For the curved line underneath the fish roll 1g (⅛oz) of yellow sugarpaste into a tapered cone shape. Attach to the underside of the fish and flatten with your finger.

7 For the fin roll 1g (⅛oz) of yellow sugarpaste into a banana shape. Mark the lines using the edge of a round cutter and attach to the top of the fish. Using the leftover yellow sugarpaste, make some small cones and dots to decorate the sides of the fish.

8 For the fish's face roll out 3g (⅛oz) of yellow sugarpaste and cut out a 2.5cm (1in) circle. Attach to the front of the fish with edible glue. Using the leftover yellow sugarpaste, make two small banana shapes for the mouth. Place one on top of the other and attach to the centre front of the head.

9 For the eyes roll two small balls of white sugarpaste and press on to either side of the head. Roll two much smaller balls of black and place on the top. Finally add two tiny balls of white to highlight the eyes. Roll 1g (⅛oz) of orange sugarpaste into two small banana shapes for the eyebrows and attach above the eyes.

10 To finish push a piece of dry spaghetti down through the centre of the splash and into the cake, leaving 2cm (¾in) showing above the splash. Slip the fish onto the spaghetti and rest it on the top of the splash. Edge the bottom of the cake with the decorative ribbon, securing it with edible glue.

You will need

Sugarpaste

* 90g (3¼oz) yellow
* 33g (1oz) grey
* 10g (⅜oz) black
* 7g (¼oz) brown
* 6g (¼oz) white

Materials

* 6.5cm (2½in) round mini cake
* Edible glue (see Recipes)
* Dry spaghetti
* Rainbow Dust: metallic silver
* Clear alcohol
* Confectioners' glaze

Equipment

* 6.5cm (2½in) Silverwood round mini cake pans
* 6.5cm (2½in) round silver cake card
* Round cutters: 7cm (2¾in), 2.5cm (1in), 1.5cm (½in)
* Basic tool kit (see General Equipment)

F1 Champion

1 To cover the cake roll out the yellow sugarpaste to an even 5mm (⅛in) strip to go around the outside of the prepared cake, finishing with a neat seam at the back. Roll out 28g (1oz) of grey sugarpaste, cut out a 7cm (2¾in) circle and set the leftover paste aside. Attach to the top of the cake. Roll 4g (⅛oz) of black sugarpaste into a thin strip to edge the grey circle. Attach the cake to the cake card and trim if there is any card showing.

2 For the flags roll 3g (⅛oz) of black sugarpaste into a thin strip measuring 12cm (4¾in), cut in half and attach to the front of the cake in a crossed position. Roll out 6g (¼oz) of white sugarpaste and cut out two 2.5cm (1in) squares.

3 For the chequered pattern roll out the remaining black sugarpaste into a thin strip and cut into small squares. Attach to the white flags and secure to the front of the cake with edible glue.

4 For the trophy roll out 7g (¼oz) of brown sugarpaste to a 1cm (⅜in) thickness. Cut out one 2.5cm (1in) circle and one 1.5cm (½in) circle. Attach the smaller circle to the centre of the larger one to make the base. Roll 1g (⅛oz) of grey sugarpaste into a sausage shape 2.5cm (1in) long. Push a piece of dry spaghetti down through the centre, leaving a little showing at one end to push into the base. Roll 3g (⅛oz) of grey sugarpaste into a ball. Push the rounded end of tool no.3 into the ball and smooth around it to form the cup. Attach the cup to the top of the stem.

5 For the trophy handles and name plate roll two thin laces of grey sugarpaste and shape into two scroll shapes for the handles. Attach to either side of the trophy with edible glue. Cut out a small rectangle using the remaining grey sugarpaste and attach to the front of the base.

6 To finish paint the grey parts of the trophy with a mixture of metallic silver dust and a little clear alcohol. Paint the trophy and all the black parts of the design with confectioners' glaze.

You will need

Sugarpaste

* 140g (5oz) green
* 27g (1oz) brown
* 10g (⅜oz) white
* 2g (⅛oz) orange

Materials

* 5cm (2in) square mini cake
* Edible glue (see Recipes)
* Dry spaghetti

Equipment

* 5cm (2in) Silverwood square mini cake pans
* 7.5cm (3in) square silver cake card
* 6cm (2⅜in) square cutter
* Crimper (oval pattern)
* Wide flower former
* Basic tool kit (see General Equipment)

Football Frenzy . . . .

1 To cover the cake roll out the green sugarpaste to an even 5mm (⅛in) thickness and cut out five 6cm (2⅜in) squares. Attach to each side and to the top of the prepared cake. Using a crimper, mark the design down each join at the side and around the top (see Crimpers). Attach the cake to the cake card and trim if there is any card showing.

2 For the lines on the top of the cake thinly roll out 5g (¼oz) of white sugarpaste. Cut a length to go down the middle of the cake then form a cross at the centre.

3 For the football roll the brown sugarpaste into an oval shape. Narrow the ends more to achieve the correct shape. Place the football inside a wide flower former to preserve the shape. Thinly roll out 5g (¼oz) of white sugarpaste, cut two thin strips and place them side-by-side on top of the ball. Cut a further strip into seven short lengths to make the laces. Add a curved strip to each end of the ball, going halfway around.

4 For the kick-off tee roll the orange sugarpaste into a short oval shape. Attach this to the centre of the cross on top of the cake.

5 To finish take a length of dry spaghetti and push it into the cake at an angle to support the ball, leaving at least 4cm (1½in) showing at the top. Slip the ball over the spaghetti and secure to the tee with edible glue.

You will need

Sugarpaste

★ 120g (4¼oz) light brown
★ 55g (2oz) blue
★ 25g (⅞oz) white

Materials

★ 6.5cm (2½in) round mini cake
★ Edible glue (see Recipes)
★ Black liquid food colour
★ Chestnut paste food colour
★ Dry spaghetti
★ Rainbow Dust: jewel
   sky blue glitter
★ Confectioners' glaze

Equipment

★ 6.5cm (2½in) Silverwood
   round mini cake pans
★ 7cm (2¾in) round
   silver cake card
★ Star cutters: 7cm (2¾in),
   3cm (1¼in), 2cm (¾in)
★ Flower former
★ Basic tool kit (see
   General Equipment)

Shooting Hoops

1 **To cover the cake** mix together the white and light brown sugarpaste to make a cream shade. Roll out to an even 5mm (⅛in) thickness and cover the prepared cake, trimming the edges neatly. Attach the cake to the cake card and trim if there is any card showing. Set the leftover paste aside for the basketball.

2 **For the stars** roll out the blue sugarpaste, cut out one 7cm (2¾in) star and attach to the top of the cake with edible glue, then cut out one 3cm (1¼in) and four 2cm (¾in) stars to decorate the side of the cake. Dust the stars with jewel sky blue glitter dust.

3 **For the basketball** add some chestnut paste food colour into 35g (1¼oz) of the leftover cream sugarpaste. Roll into a very smooth ball and, using tool no.4, mark a line right across the ball both vertically and horizontally, to mark it into quarters. Then mark an oval shape on either side. Place the ball inside a flower former to dry, as this will keep the round shape. Using a fine paintbrush, go over the lines with black liquid food colour and allow to dry.

4 **To finish** push a piece of dry spaghetti down through the centre of the cake, leaving 2cm (¾in) showing at the top. Slip the basketball over the spaghetti and secure with edible glue. Paint the ball with confectioners' glaze to make it shine.

Suppliers

UK

Berisfords Ribbons
PO Box 2, Thomas Street,
Congleton, Cheshire CW12 1EF
+44 (0) 1260 274011
office@berisfords-ribbons.co.uk
www.berisfords-ribbons.co.uk
Ribbons – see website for stockists

The British Sugarcraft Guild
Wellington House, Messeter Place,
London SE9 5DP
+44 (0) 20 8859 6943
nationaloffice@bsguk.org
www.bsguk.org
*Exhibitions, courses,
members' benefits*

The Cake Decorating Company
2b Triumph Road,
Nottingham NG7 2GA
+44 (0) 115 822 4521
info@thecakedecoratingcompany.co.uk
www.thecakedecoratingcompany.co.uk
For all cake-decorating supplies

Maisie Parrish
Maisie's World, 840 High Lane, Chell,
Stoke on Trent, Staffordshire ST6 6HG
+44 (0) 1782 876090
maisie.parrish@ntlworld.com
www.maisieparrish.com
*Novelty cake decorating, one-to-
one tuition, workshops and demos*

Pinch of Sugar
1256 Leek Road, Abbey Hulton,
Stoke on Trent ST2 8BP
+44 (0) 1782 570557
sales@pinchofsugar.co.uk
www.pinchofsugar.co.uk
*Bakeware, tools, boards and
boxes, sugarcraft supplies, ribbons,
colours, decorations and candles*

Renshaws
Crown Street, Liverpool L8 7RF
+44 (0) 870 870 6954
enquiries@renshaw-nbf.co.uk
www.renshaw-nbf.co.uk
*Caramels, Regalice sugarpastes,
marzipans and compounds*

Alan Silverwood Ltd
Ledsam House, Ledsam Street,
Birmingham B16 8DN
+44 (0) 121 454 3571
sales@alan-silverwood.co.uk
www.alansilverwood.co.uk
Bakeware, multi-mini cake pans

Rainbow Dust
Unit 3, Cuerden Green Mill,
Lostock Hall, Preston PR5 5LP
+44 (0) 1772 322335
info@rainbowdust.co.uk
www.rainbowdust.co.uk
*Dust food colours, pens and
edible cake decorations*

USA

All In One Bake Shop
8566 Research Blvd, Austin, TX 78758
+1 512 371 3401
info@allinonebakeshop.com
www.allinonebakeshop.com
*Cake-making and
decorating supplies*

Caljava International Ltd
Northridge, CA 91324
+1 800 207 2750
sales@caljavaonline.com
www.caljavaonline.com
*Cake-decorating supplies
and classes*

European Cake Gallery
844 North Crowley Road,
Crowley, TX 76036
+1 817 297 2240
info@thesugarart.com
www.europeancakegallery.us
www.thesugarart.com
Cake and sugarcraft supplies

Global Sugar Art
7 Plattsburgh Plaza,
Plattsburgh, NY 12901
+1 800 420 6088
info@globalsugarart.com
www.globalsugarart.com
Everything sugarcraft

**Wilton School of Cake
Decorating and Confectionery Art**
7511 Lemont Road, Darien, IL 60561
+1 630 985 6077
wiltonschool@wilton.com
www.wilton.com
Bakeware, supplies and tuition

CANADA

Golda's Kitchen Inc.
2885 Argentia Road, Unit 6, Mississauga,
Ontario L5N 8G6
+1 905 816 9995
golda@goldaskitchen.com
www.goldaskitchen.com
*Bakeware, cake-decorating
and sugarcraft supplies*

NETHERLANDS

Liesbeth's Taarten Atelier
Handekenskruid 38,
4635 BJ Huijbergen
+ 31 (0) 6 1896 2997
info@liesbethstaartenatelier.nl
www.liesbethstaartenatelier.nl
Cake-decorating supplies and classes

SPAIN

La Tienda Americana
Paseo de San Francisco de Sales 5
28003 Madrid
+34 91 311 9438
info@latiendaamericana.es
www.latiendaamericana.es
Bakeware, cake-decorating supplies and tuition

AUSTRALIA

Cakes Around Town Pty Ltd
2/12 Subury Street,
Darra, Queensland 4076
+61 (0) 731 608 728
info@cakesaroundtown.com.au
www.cakesaroundtown.com.au
Cake-making and decorating supplies

Iced Affair
53 Church Street,
Camperdown, NSW 2050
+61 (0) 295 193 679
icedaffair@iprimus.com.au
www.icedaffair.com.au
Cake-making and decorating supplies

Planet Cake
106 Beattie Street,
Balmain, NSW 2041
+61 (0) 298 103 843
info@planetcake.com.au
www.planetcake.com.au
Cake-making and decorating supplies

Acknowledgments

My grateful thanks to Renshaws for generously supplying me with their wonderful range of readymade sugarpaste. The beautiful colours in their range have helped me to create so many lovely characters and make this book outstanding. The photography by Simon Whitmore brings to life the magical quality of each project, so beautifully staged by Victoria Marks. So much encouragement and help has been given to me in the making of this book by the editorial staff of David & Charles, particularly by James Brooks and Jeni Hennah, with my special thanks to Ame Verso for her brilliant editorial touch.

About the Author

Maisie Parrish is completely self-taught and her characters have a unique quality that is instantly recognizable and much copied. Over the last few years, she has been very busy travelling to many different countries, teaching and demonstrating her skills. She was honoured to be the prime demonstrator for the New Zealand Cake Guild, and became an honourary member of the Victoria Cake Guild in Australia. She is a tutor at The Wilton School of Cake Decorating in Chicago, The International School of Culinary Education in New York, Caljava International School of Cake Decorating in California and Squires Kitchen International School of Sugarcraft in England to mention but a few. She is also an accredited demonstrator for the British Sugarcraft Guild.

Her fans travel thousands of miles to visit her home studio in Stoke on Trent, England, for a chance to be taught by the master. People find it difficult to believe she never actually bakes cakes for anyone, she considers herself to be a sugar artist who can visit as many as three countries in a month.

Maisie has enjoyed several television appearances, including *The Good Food Show* and *QVC*, and is the author of ten books and star of three DVDs. Further examples of her work can be seen on her website, **www.maisieparrish.com** where she welcomes you into **Maisie's World**.

Templates

To download full-size printable
PDFs of these templates, go to:
www.bakeme.com/page/templates.

Whole Nine Yards Number templates

Hobby-Mad Minis
Baseball Classic flag template

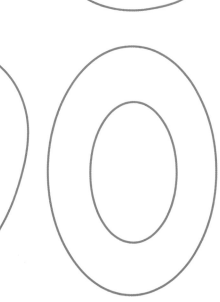

1 2 3
4 5 6
7 8 9 0

Index

A DAVID & CHARLES BOOK
© F&W Media International, LTD 2012

David & Charles is an imprint of F&W Media International, LTD
Brunel House, Forde Close, Newton Abbot, TQ12 4PU, UK

F&W Media International, LTD is a subsidiary of F+W Media, Inc.
4700 East Galbraith Road, Cincinnati, OH 45236

First published in the UK and USA in 2012
Digital edition published in 2012

ISBN-13: 978-1-4463-0162-3 paperback
ISBN-10: 1-4463-0162-1 paperback

ISBN-13: 978-1-4463-5583-1 e-pub
ISBN-10: 1-4463-5583-7 e-pub

ISBN-13: 978-1-4463-5582-4 PDF
ISBN-10: 1-4463-5582-9 PDF

Paperback edition printed in China by RR Donnelley
for F&W Media International, LTD
Brunel House, Forde Close, Newton Abbot, TQ12 4PU, UK

10 9 8 7 6 5 4 3 2 1

Publisher: Alison Myer
Commissioning Editor: Jennifer Fox-Proverbs
Desk Editor: Jeni Hennah
Project Editor: Ame Verso
Senior Designer: Victoria Marks
Photographer: Simon Whitmore
Senior Production Controller: Kelly Smith

F+W Media, Inc. publishes high quality books on a wide
range of subjects. For more great book ideas visit:
www.rucraft.co.uk